C000163096

Harold Pinter'

'All you have do is shut up and enjoy the hospitality.'

– Terry

Harold Pinter's *Party Time* (1991) is an extraordinary distillation of the playwright's key concerns. Pulsing with political anger, it marks a stepping stone on Pinter's path from iconic dramatist of existential unease to Nobel Prize-winning poet of human rights.

G. D. White situates this underrated play within a recognisably 'Pinteresque' landscape of ambiguous, brittle social drama while also recognising its particularity: *Party Time* is haunted by Augusto Pinochet's right-wing coup against Salvador Allende's democratically elected government in Chile.

This book considers *Party Time* and its confederate plays in the dual context of Pinter's literary career and burgeoning international concern with human rights and freedom of expression, contrasting his uneasy relationship with the UK's powerful elite with the worldwide acclaim for his dramatic eviscerations of power.

'All you have do is shut up and enjoy the hospitality.'

G. D. White is Professor of Drama at the University of Roehampton, London.

The Fourth Wall

The Fourth Wall series is a growing collection of short books on famous plays. Its compact format perfectly suits the kind of fresh, engaging criticism that brings a play to life.

Each book in this series selects one play or musical as its subject and approaches it from an original angle, seeking to shed light on an old favourite or break new ground on a modern classic. These lively, digestible books are a must for anyone looking for new ideas on the major works of modern theatre.

Also available in this series:

J. M. Synge's *The Playboy of the Western World* by Christopher Collins
Heiner Müller's *The Hamletmachine* by David Barnett
Lerner and Loewe's *My Fair Lady* by Keith Garebian
Samuel Beckett's *Krapp's Last Tape* by Daniel Sack
Thornton Wilder's *The Skin of Our Teeth* by Kyle Gillette

Coming soon:

Georg Büchner's *Woyzeck* by Karoline Gritzner
Benjamin Britten's *Peter Grimes* by Sam Kinchin-Smith
J. M. Barrie's *Peter Pan* by Lucie Sutherland
Sondheim and Wheeler's *Sweeney Todd* by Aaron Thomas
Errol John's *Moon on a Rainbow Shawl* by Lynnette Goddard
Caryl Churchill's *Far Away* by Dan Rebellato
August Wilson's *Joe Turner's Come and Gone* by Ladrica Menson-Furr
Tim Crouch's *An Oak Tree* by Catherine Love
Rogers and Hammerstein's *The Sound of Music* by Julian Woolford

Harold Pinter's
Party Time

G. D. White

Routledge
Taylor & Francis Group

LONDON AND NEW YORK

First published 2016
by Routledge
2 Park Square, Milton Park, Abingdon, Oxon OX14 4RN

and by Routledge
711 Third Avenue, New York, NY 10017

Routledge is an imprint of the Taylor & Francis Group, an informa business

British Library Cataloguing-in-Publication Data
A catalogue record for this book is available from
the British Library

Library of Congress Cataloguing-in-Publication Data
A catalog record for this title has been requested

ISBN: 9781138677258 (pbk)
ISBN: 9781315559612 (ebk)

Typeset in Bembo
by Out of House Publishing

For Debra, (Community Protection Warden) . . .

Contents

1   Incident at dinner   1

2   *Party Time*   25

3   Wentworth days   42

      Index   65

Incident at dinner

'All you have to do is shut up and enjoy the hospitality[.]'[1]

In 1985 the American playwright Arthur Miller was the guest at a reception held by the American Ambassador to Turkey while on a visit to the country on behalf of the writer's organisation PEN International. Miller had made the journey with the British playwright Harold Pinter, and the two of them had been sobered by what they had heard from relatives of writers imprisoned under the ruling military dictatorship. Raising concerns at the reception about the treatment of political prisoners, Pinter got into an argument with one of the guests over the use of torture in Turkish prisons.[2] In a later discussion with the Ambassador, who sought to articulate the US administration's support for a Turkish government whose country bordered Soviet Russia, Pinter was told that 'you have to bear in mind the political reality, the diplomatic reality, the military reality'. 'The reality I've been referring to', Pinter replied, 'is that of electric current on your genitals'.[3]

Pinter described the incident in an essay titled 'Arthur Miller's Socks', written for the American playwright's 80th birthday. In it Pinter contrasts strongly the two writers' approaches to the same question on this visit – how to confront oppressive power? For Miller, the answer came in a direct but measured use of his guest status during his invited speech, which considered how support for an authoritarian regime clashed with the United States' declared commitment to democratic values. For Pinter the answer came in taking a different kind of opportunity – to make a point, employing the directness of the irascible argument, the provocation of outrage, the flouting of convention.

The moment of the possible confrontation between power and the relatively powerless, between authority and those who hold that authority to account is quintessentially dramatic. It demands that the figure who asserts the essential truth of a situation speak that truth to power, and step across a line of politeness and evasion, of obfuscation, or of refusal. It is at the heart of drama from Sophocles' *Antigone* to Shakespeare's *King Lear*, to Miller's own *The Crucible*. As I write, the British media has been focused on the visit of the Chinese President Xi Jinping to London among a flurry of trade deals. The issue of quite when or how the delicate negotiation of the Chinese government's human rights record might be conducted, and who – British Prime Minister or British leader of the opposition – might raise it has been widely picked over, but it is unlikely that such a drama of diplomatic confrontation will be played out in any public setting. That powerplay is likely to be conducted backstage, in diplomacy's private antechambers.

Harold Pinter's 1991 play *Party Time* focuses on this kind of moment in a portrait of the private social interactions of the powerful. The play takes place at a party where we observe the small talk of a privileged group. At first hearing that small talk is all about what binds the group together – the membership of an exclusive club, the enjoyment of particular leisure activities, the approval of a certain kind of strong governmental – and personal – behaviour. At the same time the small talk aims at the avoidance, until the party's celebratory climax, of some kind of nasty business that has been going on out in the streets. This is revealed to have been a round-up, a restoration of order. The play shows us a gathering in which the codes of conduct and the holding of power are all based in the performance of language, and it is through the maintenance of languages' ability to control, cajole, mask and flatter that power is gained and withheld among the group. And yet, in the calm of the elite surroundings, there are persistent notes of dissent and unease, in particular a question from a guest that continually threatens to upset the even tone of the gathering.

DUSTY: What's happened to Jimmy?[4]

Party Time is an exploration of what binds a power elite together and of what threatens to fragment it, and it is in the recurrence of the question of what happened to Jimmy – and of whether what happened is something that can or will be talked about – that Pinter's play gains its nightmarish effect.

The wave of largely non-violent revolutions that swept eastern Europe in 1989 is characterised by images of power discomfited and forced to account for itself, from East German border guards responding with bemusement to the crowds of demonstrators demanding to cross the Berlin Wall into the West to the uncomprehending concern of Nikolai Ceauşescu faced by disruption and booing from a crowd in front of the presidential palace in Bucharest in the same year that signalled the end of his regime. Pinter's play first appears in the aftermath of these moments, premiering at the Almeida theatre in Islington, London in 1991. By making such clear reference to political circumstances the play seemed to be part of a shift of focus, somewhat out of step with the body of work that had built Pinter's reputation. The play did, however, share obvious concerns with examining the broad questions of power, authority and human rights that had become an explicit part of his writing since 1984's *One for the Road*. That piece depicted a brutal but urbane interrogator destroying a family of dissidents in a dance of menace and threatened violence. Along with its successor, 1987's *Mountain Language*, in which a group of dispossessed people are intimidated by an army of the powerful, the work suggested Pinter's emerging concern with political oppression. Irving Wardle's review of *Party Time* indicates how it works both to anatomise a way of speaking and to illustrate that this appeared to be a new synthesis in the playwright's work:

> He has at last constructed a bridge between his dramatic world and the world of his political conscience. *Party Time* may be unlocalized, but it reflects the reported iniquities of Africa and Latin America in the perspective of a London he knows inside out.[5]

In a 1970 speech on being awarded the West German Shakespeare prize Pinter famously spoke of how a remark he once made about his work had come back to haunt him:

> Once, many years ago, I found myself engaged uneasily in a public discussion on the theatre. Someone asked me

what my work was 'about'. I replied with no thought at all and merely to frustrate this line of enquiry: 'The weasel under the cocktail cabinet'.[6]

Whether intentional or not, Pinter's remark captured in metaphor that mixture of social sophistication and hidden violent unease that characterised his work from the 1950s territory of *The Room*; through the series of domestic interiors that mark his trio of plays, *The Birthday Party*, *The Caretaker* and *The Homecoming*; to the chilly middle-class landscapes of the 1970s dramas, including *Old Times*, *No Man's Land* and *Betrayal*. The shifting sands of this territory were his habitual dramatic landscape, and the sense of ambiguity and menace that characterised them gave rise to the coining of a critical commonplace for his style – the 'Pinteresque'. This term stood for the portrayal of a world in which lurking, upsetting dangers broke the social surface to raise ambiguities and uncertainties in human identity and relations; successive plays featured characters bursting, like Lenny in *The Homecoming*, into moments of violent, expressionistic savagery in language, if not in deed. That Pinter subsequently regretted ever using the 'weasel' phrase did not lessen its usefulness for readers seeking meaning, teachers discussing the work with their pupils or directors and actors hunting through the language and uncertain action of his plays to fix interpretation.

Pinter had already made a remark that was to prove similarly unhelpful for him. His reluctance in an earlier stage of his career to offer up explanations of his work and methods in interview had led to the collected published editions of his plays generally containing an introduction taken from a public lecture. These remain some of the most compelling

outlinings of dramatic writing in print, but, like the territory
of the Pinteresque, they also contain challenges and contradictions. In the 1962 speech to the National Student Drama
Festival, which was initially published as 'Writing for the
Theatre,' the introduction to his first volume of *Collected
Plays*, Pinter stated 'What I write has no obligation to anything other than itself',[7] an apparent disavowal of the theatre's
commitment to engage socially. Again this provided a critical context for the consideration of Pinter's work. It was not
to be read for a political subtext. There were no puzzles of
attribution, or direct correspondences between the predicament of a character and the political climate of the times in
which the play was written. If a particular production were
to suggest political resonances might be drawn – if, for example, Stanley's persecution in *The Birthday Party* were explicitly
staged as a metaphor for Eastern Bloc doublethink – this was
a by-product of the universality of the subject matter being
explored, not a direct reference to external reality or the key
to a system of interpretation for the work. Yet if Pinter were
to regret the statement about the weasel, how much more was
he to regret, and to challenge and revise, this statement about
the theatre's obligation? By 1984 Pinter was working on *One
for the Road*, the first of a series of plays that was to usher in
an era of very direct 'political' writing, in which the modes
of address, the subject matter and the styles of his work were
to make clear, if tangential, references to particular political
environments and circumstances – shifting yes, metaphorical
of course, but written by all accounts from the understanding
of specific events. In the conversation between Pinter and the
publisher Nick Hern that prefaces a 1985 edition of the play,
Pinter makes clear that the apparent absence of politics in
the preceding period was not quite as it may have appeared,

and that political acts and political concerns had always been deeply embedded in his life and writing.[8]

Perhaps it was the trip to Turkey, his engagement with PEN International, and his communication with writers such as the Czechoslovakian dramatist Václav Havel whose political circumstances restricted their freedom of expression that brought home to Pinter the potential of writing, the exploration of language, and the taking of a position of dissent as issues that could be explored dramatically. Or perhaps the poetic images of lives arrested and decayed in the trilogy of *Old Times*, *No Man's Land*, and *Betrayal* had already begun to suggest a need to shift the focus away from the landscapes of the interpersonal toward the public. Whichever, it is documented in Pinter's obituary by his biographer Michael Billington[9] that in 1973 Pinter was persuaded by theatre associates (including the playwright David Mercer and the actor Peggy Ashcroft) to speak out against the coup led by General Augusto Pinochet that overthrew Salvador Allende's democratically elected left-wing government, a foundational moment in his understanding of the ways in which the spoken and the written might clash with the extreme exercise of power.

As a student I spent a good deal of time at the repertory cinemas of London – buildings like the Rio in Dalston, the Everyman in Hampstead, and the Scala in Kings Cross – on a cinema circuit that predated the DVD age and that provided a space in which cinema's canon of classics, arthouse, and cult films were recycled long after their initial theatrical release. It was at the Rio that I watched the Costa-Gavras film *Missing*, starring Jack Lemmon and Sissy Spacek. Set in Chile after the 1973 coup, the film deals with the 'real-life' story of Joyce and Ed Horman, wife and father of an

American journalist, Charles Horman, who disappeared in the aftermath of Pinochet's crackdown. At the time the film was engrossing, enraging, and enlightening. It followed the journey from innocence to experience of the Christian Scientist father as he grew steadily more aware of the injustice of that coup and of his own government's apparent complicity in the events that led to the death of his son. Horman also grew to recognise the heroism of his daughter-in-law – Spacek plays a character called Beth who is based on the Joyce Horman of the real events – and the moral strength of the son he had taken to be a waster. I've not seen the film since, but at the time it changed my view of politics, in part because of its moral intensity, the clear depiction of a link between political expediency and callous human cruelty. I've no idea what I would make of *Missing* if I saw it now – and if it's anything like Costa-Gavras' later *Music Box*, another admirably intentioned film, I suspect I might find it rather less compelling – but it had its effect at the time. Since then I have become more sceptical of direct political messages and solutions. I am not easily led to see art as a substitute for life, or polemic as a substitute for complexity, and yet *Missing* stays as a watershed in both my understanding of what art can do, and my understanding of the extremity of what power will do if it finds itself convinced of a threat to its dominance.

In Chile 9/11 has a different historical resonance from that of the same date in the USA. For Chileans, the 9/11 of 2001 was already a marker of historical trauma, the day when the Chilean parliament building, La Moneda, in the capital, Santiago, was bombarded by the British-built Hawker Hunter jets of that part of the Chilean air force which was loyal to the uprising mounted by a military faction led by General

Augusto Pinochet Duarte. The coup was a direct, violent, and bloody response to Allende's left-wing social and economic policies and it resulted in the death of the President. In the aftermath, and in the years that followed, it also resulted in the death, torture, and imprisonment of thousands of supposed dissidents; communists; Marxists; trade unionists; liberals; sympathisers; men, women, and children; American dissidents; foreign émigrés; and, as we shall see, British and Spanish citizens. As Andy Beckett makes clear in his brilliant dissection of the history of British–Chilean relations and of the impact of this coup, *Pinochet in Piccadilly*, the aftermath is of particular note here. What happened in and after the coup was hidden, a matter of intense secrecy and repression by a military government. Opponents of the regime simply disappeared into a hidden network of prisons, barracks, hospitals, and industrial sites, which became the apparatus of oppression. And the reality of what happened in this period only begins to emerge through committed, dogged detailing, research, and representation by dissenters, survivors, and relatives of the missing. Outside Chile much of this coalesces around art and culture – including Costa-Gavras' film, made almost a decade later, and a flurry of publicity around the death in the coup's aftermath of the polemicist songwriter Victor Jara (which results in a Bob Dylan-headlined support concert at Madison Square Garden in 1974). It is also explored in the campaigning work of organisations like Amnesty International, whose commitment to a concept of human rights and free expression that transcends political particularities articulated a space in which the concerns of the unaligned artist and the victim of repression might combine.[10] By the mid-1980s, Pinter's writing had begun to trace an explicit commitment to these forms of political engagement.

In 1978 I raced home from school to the most exciting televisual experience of my life. This was the first full-scale televised World Cup that my football-obsessed imagination had been able to engage with. British television was a live football desert in 1978, but now, the World Cup in Argentina was kicking off with an evening game between Poland and the current champions, West Germany. Never mind that it was one of the dullest matches in the history of the sport, a tense 0–0 draw between two bitter rivals – this was the beginning of a feast of international football spread over a whole month. And it was played out with all the gloriously distant otherness of 1970s international technology: a commentary down a phone line, sound and pictures appearing to be broadcast from the moon.

A kilometre from the Estadio Monumental, in which this unpromising curtain-raiser was played, across a highway and a couple of sports-club fields, stood a building of which the average television viewer in Argentina, let alone Britain, would have been entirely ignorant. Yet in the Naval Mechanics' School, even as the World Cup matches kicked off, the Argentinian military had been and were torturing and murdering those identified as their political opponents – left-wing students, sympathisers, trade unionists, campaigners, and their benighted families, friends, and acquaintances – rounded up in orchestrated campaigns by the military junta that had taken power in a coup in 1976. Five thousand people passed through this interrogation centre. Of these, just 150 survived. The rest were drugged and then shot or, in many cases, flown, still drugged, in aircraft over the Atlantic from which they were pushed to their deaths. Many children, born to those imprisoned, were taken away for adoption by families connected to the ruling military, a process that is currently still being reversed as these now adult children discover the secrets of their true parentage. The electronic texture of the remoteness of Argentina was a captivating element in the representation of the World Cup, but a deeply disturbing one in the context of international politics. I recall no commentary, remark, or suggestion during the tournament that indicated that there was any form of political unrest in Argentina. I knew that there was a reputation for violence among Argentinian football fans that the violence of supporters was of an order more intense and extreme even than in hooligan-afflicted England, and that the moats built around the pitches in the larger stadia were there to prevent supporter invasion. But I knew nothing of the politics of the country. As the tournament progressed, the home team's 6–0 win over Peru in their final group match had the feel of something suspicious, 6 being exactly the goal tally that the team needed to progress (though this also tallied with the sporting xenophobia through which British commentators tended to tar all international football as being prone to cheating). But my understanding, as a reasonably aware schoolboy, was that the biggest tragedy of the World Cup was Scotland's hubristic exit. As a 2002 documentary on the context of the Dutch football team's journey to the final makes clear, the political reality in the country was known, or at least investigated, by those who felt it their duty, but for the most part a veil of secrecy was maintained over these events.[11] Argentina's dictatorship was determined to ensure that no-one spoiled the party.

First staged in London at the Lyric Studio, Hammersmith in 1984, Pinter's short play *One for the Road* is written in the aftermath of that World-Cup-era repression in Argentina, a foundational part of the 'national reorganisation' that the 1976 coup brought about. A series of scenes depict the interrogation of a man, a woman, and a child by Nicolas, an urbane, menacing figure whose manner switches between apparent civility and viciousness in a moment. Nicolas is plausible and restrained but his manner and attitude conceal a sadistic concern with the destruction of those whose values and attitudes collide with his own and those of the powers he represents. The play makes clear the family relationship among the three prisoners, and the process by which an interrogation might switch focus from one to another in order to reach its goal – the breaking of the man by his interrogator. Without direct reference to a circumstance, Pinter anatomises the process of psychological terror that the Argentine regime exploited. The humiliation and dehumanisation of the prisoners of the Naval Mechanics' School was completed by the removal of their children, by the denial of their families' right to know anything of their whereabouts or fate, sometimes through forced deception – female prisoners taken out for family visits, or even to macabre city-centre meals with army recruits: events designed to suggest that all is well and positive. In *One for the Road*, the breaking of the male interrogatee, Victor, is achieved by Nicolas' gradual erosion of his humanity through the threats that follow the pleasantries and through the targeting of the two figures of most importance to him: his wife, Gila, and child, Nicky. Both of these figures appear on stage; both face the mixture of charm and brutality that Nicolas exudes; both watch his ritual drink, arming him for the next onslaught. Gila is subject to repeated rape. Victor is tortured, left hardly able to speak. In the final scene he is told that he is to be released, and that Gila will follow him 'in about a week', the implication being that her torment will continue at the hands of her captors. As Victor struggles to ask what has happened to his son, Nicholas pretends not to be able to hear him, before finally Victor is able to expel the words, to which Nicholas responds brutally:

NICHOLAS: Your son? Oh, don't worry about him. He was a little prick.[12]
VICTOR straightens and stares at NICHOLAS

The stage direction registers Victor's motion as a gesture of resistance, even in this unbearable extremis.

One for the Road emerged in response to specific political circumstances, but its subject matter was both particular and universal. The play employs the codes and manners of English middle-class civility, apparently removing direct reference to suggest a generality of application. Yet the process of interrogation that it provides a vision of is universal. The experience of post-Allende Chile, the Chile of Pinochet's dictatorship, of the military juntas of Argentina and Paraguay, of the Lubyankas and Gulags of the Soviet Union, of the Gestapo cells of the Second World War echo through the play. It spoke to its audience with visceral pointedness. Andy Beckett records an interview, many years after the events, with Sergio Rueda, a Chilean émigré living in England who had been arrested immediately after Pinochet's coup and taken to a large period house on the outskirts of Santiago. There,

blindfolded, Rueda was informed that his wife, who was three months pregnant, and his daughter, who was now three years old, had also been arrested. Two names were read out to him, and he was asked their whereabouts . . . If Rueda was uncooperative, the Captain continued, 'You have to understand, I have all my powers from my

General Pinochet to do whatever I want with you and
your family.'[13]

The account of the torture that follows is utterly harrowing.
It is a moment such as that faced by the blindfolded Rueda
that Pinter captures.

In 1988 I sat in a room in the University of Sussex in
Brighton as Harold Pinter read from his new play *Mountain
Language*. I'd first encountered Pinter's work through the
frame of my sister's amused response to the opening pages of
The Birthday Party as she studied it for 'O' level, intrigued by
the register of banal exchanges between Petey and Meg over
the enjoyment of breakfast and the content of the newspaper. She was struck by the odd, off-kilter surrealism of the
exchanges between the two characters, and would regularly
perform them around the house, the playwright's portrait of
the world mixing with the banalities of our own breakfasts
and conversations. I'm not aware that I'd read or seen any
other of Pinter's work, but at that time I was often stum-
bling across TV dramas that seemed to take the familiar and
move off at a tangent, tilting the known world and making
me look at it afresh. My own first viewing came through a
1980 BBC TV production of *The Caretaker*, staring Warren
Mitchell, Kenneth Cranham, and Jonathan Pryce, shown as
I began an 'A'-level English literature course, and this also
slipped the world off its familiar hinges. The moment when
Pryce's character Mick surprises the tramp Davies, played
by Mitchell, by hoovering in the dark, and then starting an
apparently friendly conversation is now thick with the recog-
nisable techniques of Pinter's dramaturgy: the staging of the
limits of a room; the predicament of a vulnerable figure being
bamboozled by the bewildering, swiftly shifting address of a

predatory interloper; the fizzing rush of language, of comic articulacy covering menace; but at the time it came as a revelation. This writer seemed to have an acute take on a sort of grimy, ordinary life that was both articulate and inarticulate, often in the same flow of language.

Yet the Pinter who appeared a few years later at the university didn't seem to be that Pinter. This Pinter spoke in the deep, sonorous tones of the very posh, and was accompanied by his partner, Lady Antonia Fraser, and by the great and the good of the university. This posh, I was to realise, was drama-school posh, the acquired tones of the trained rep actor Pinter had once been, but I wasn't aware of that at the time. And here he was, ready to read a play, his single voice carrying all of the weight of the language. I'd had the good fortune as an undergraduate to be in tutorials with the playwright Simon Gray, close friend and long-time collaborator of Pinter's (Pinter directed first productions of many of Gray's plays). He would arrive, scowling, and, if it was after lunch, with a glass of white wine in hand. He would light up a cigarette and then begin to read us things – extracts from Larkin's prose, poems by Browning. I can still hear his voice reading the baffling opening lines of Browning's *A Toccata of Galuppi's* (who was Toccata, what's a Galuppi?); 'Oh Galuppi, Baldessaro, this is very sad to find! / I can hardly misconceive you; it would prove me deaf and blind . . .'. This seemed to be the world of the 'playwright', a posh, eyebrow-raised scepticism, and an indulgent, rich survey of the world of literature and its proponents. There was no direct reference to a particular commitment in this study, or suggestion that it should be the role of the writer to engage with a specific, politicised territory. And, anyway, how might a spoken reading indicate a 'commitment'?

What Pinter read brought the commitment. A set of short scenes, brief exchanges, gestures, and statements. The thrust of the play was clear. It did not address itself to an underclass of dispossessed Londoners, or subtly interrogate the hostilities between the genders in the rarefied surroundings of a Regent's Park mansion. It seemed to take place in a refugee camp, and while it featured the brutal harrowing of those dispossessed figures – comic interrogation rewritten as direct, uncompromising oppression of a group by another – it didn't reference a specific situation. Here the figure who intimidated was a soldier threatening a migrant with death for the crime of speaking a forbidden language. The play made clear that this language was illegitimate, that the language of the city was the dominant one, and that the figures being abused, marginalised, derided were being subjected to the brutal closing-down of their space and freedoms, both to exist and to speak. The play dramatized a community under attack, or control, its particularity being destroyed by the force of the military, with its organised, discriminatory violence.

Mountain Language consists of a series of four short scenes that seem to deal with a detention camp. In the first, a number of women wait for entry, apparently to see their detained relatives. They are treated contemptuously by the male guards, particularly for speaking the banned language of the mountain regions. In the second scene, set in the visitors' room, a guard loudly demands that an elderly woman stop using the language:

GUARD: It's forbidden. (To PRISONER) Tell her to speak the language of the capital.[14]

In the third, a young woman is led into a room to be told by the aggressive guard that there has been a mistake. She sees a hooded man who is being tortured. For a moment the voices of the young man and young woman echo over the top of the scene as the characters freeze communicating, creating a resistance that *One for the Road* had imaged in Victor's final motions. Then the torture begins again, the man collapses. The Guard uses bluff evasions to mask the deliberate intimidation:

SERGEANT: Yes, you've come in the wrong door. It must be the computer. The computer's got a double hernia.[15]

Her arrival in the room is no mistake. In the final scene a Prisoner sits, shivering, and the Old Woman sits near him. The Prisoner has blood on his face. The Guard tells the Prisoner that the rules have changed, and that the Old Woman can speak in her language now. The arbitrary change is of a piece with the other rules in the camp. The Prisoner talks to the Old Woman, addressing her as 'Mother'. She does not respond. The banning of language is unnecessary. Its destruction has been achieved by the silencing of the people who spoke it.

The inspiration for the play appears to come from the moment of Pinter's visit to Turkey. In the 1980s, the military government that had taken power in Turkey banned the use of the Kurdish language. The country's government was caught up in an uprising by the Kurdish Workers' Party, the PKK. This insurgency, fought in the south-east of the country, mirroring the violence between the Kurdish forces and those of the regime of Saddam Hussein in Northern Iraq, was ended by a PKK ceasefire at the end of the century, but broke out in a further conflict in 2004, since which time ceasefire and conflict have alternated. Throughout the period the Kurdish language has been a subject of great controversy, with severe restrictions on its use, particularly in educational and broadcasting contexts. These restrictions have been largely eased by an increasingly progressive Turkish state, but the significance of such prohibition as a key tool in the domination of ethnic or geographic groups is an historic given. In the time since the writing of Pinter's play the notion of quite how far national identity might be bound up in questions of language has become an established element of liberal democracy across Europe, while remaining a contentious issue throughout the same landscape. At the time of the play's first reading this felt like a moment of recognition, bringing to an audience a particular politics in a point in time when the link between an extreme situation and the art that reflects it was made clear. However, the violence of the play, largely the violence of language and threat, seemed remote and extreme. I understood the Latin American reference for *One for the Road*. I recognised that Central America resonated with the sounds of death squads and paramilitaries. I could see that the activities of secret police in states across the world were being evoked in that play's exemplar, but in the case of *Mountain Language* the topic seemed horrifying yet remote. Ethnic nationalisms across Europe were not as this, notwithstanding the violence between state and armed groups in Northern Ireland and the Basque country. Turkey remained a separate space, a nation on the fringes of the political complexities of the Middle East – Syria, Libya, Iraq, Iran – where factional and sectarian conflict shifted and seethed underneath whichever dictatorial hand held control. In such conflicts the potential for the use of extreme violence to promote social control seemed undeniable, and if Saddam Hussein was gassing Kurdish villagers in northern Iraq just as Turkey was restricting the human rights of its Kurdish population, then Pinter's portrayal of an oppressive violence seemed reasonable.

Yet, as Drew Milne makes clear, the characteristics of Pinter's work should caution us against reading it as direct political commentary. Milne points out that 'Pinter's concrete images suggest that the language of political abstraction needs to be resisted'.[16] The plays themselves echo particular circumstances, but their dramatic technique challenges the distancing terms and definitions of political discourse. It is in the welding of a familiar dramaturgy to the dynamics of torture, oppression, and the self-projection of power that, as Milne suggests, Pinter's work gains a poetic resonance and, for Robert Gordon, a prophetic power.[17] As the former Yugoslavia was torn apart by interstate and interethnic conflict in the 1990s, and the degree of barbarism employed by the leaders, armed forces, and militias of the warring groups became clearer, so *Mountain Language*'s unblinking directness began to look less extreme. That the 'others' might, in this play, have been reduced to ciphers, figures to be pushed around and physically and verbally abused, and that such atrocity might bear the hallmarks of absurdity – one woman complains that a dog has bitten her; the Guard tells her that if she wants to make a complaint she has to give him its name – seemed like a nightmarish projection of the extremity of conflict. The Yugoslav Civil War brought massacre and ethnic cleansing to public view – Croat, Serb, and Bosnian Muslim each victim to and suspect in war crimes; a litany of town, village, sports ground, cultural centre, shoe factory, or collective farm attacked, shelled, turned into a detention centre or a site of killing. While political abstractions began to mask and motivate particular atrocities, the intensity of the conflict made Pinter's *Mountain Language* vision look restrained, requiring the appearance of the vivid, explosive surrealism of a Sarah Kane to attempt its capture.

In the aftermath of the writing of *Mountain Language* the specificity of Pinter's commitment became clearer. However, the place of Pinter in the public consciousness after the writing of these three plays and their associated texts – the short *The New World Order* and the longer, profound mediation on past horror, *Ashes to Ashes* – is intriguing, and contradictory. In Britain the playwright, whose work had always been the subject of a range of parody, became an increasingly regular target for commentators unhappy with this presumptuous mix of art and outspoken politics. From such perspectives the playwright's linking of dramatic myth and metaphor to concrete political commentary appeared as an awkward and embarrassing extension of his characteristic areas of exploration. The directness and emotiveness of Pinter's public interventions in political debate – most notably the establishing of the 20 June writers' group to discuss the contemporary political situation – often provoked derision, and frequently on the grounds of a lack of taste and proportion. To caricature the caricature, Pinter was seen as the ultimate 'champagne socialist', a luvvie with a far-back accent and an absurdly short fuse. At the same time the fact that Pinter's plays had grown shorter and more apparently restricted in subject and structure (the *Faber Collected Plays 4* volume, spanning twelve years, contains twelve texts written between 1978 and 1990, only one of which is 'full length') led to suggestions that Pinter's was a muse gone to seed, a combative and insightful theatrical imagination turned now to simplistic political solutions to the elegant conundrums it had previously explored. The British parodist Craig Brown produced an acute study of Pinter's own assertive 'voice', catching with a satiric eye the tendency to aggrandising overstatement that could undermine Pinter's engagement with the political world outside his dramas.[18] There is no escaping the pungency of Brown's satires, or the sense of Pinter as a figure trapped by his parodist's mining of the recurrent patterns and tropes in what he has to say, and Brown became something of a hate figure for Pinter – a fact from which Brown made great, and amusing, capital.[19]

And yet, internationally, Pinter's reputation had never been higher. In the works staged and published between *One for the Road* and *Ashes to Ashes*, Pinter seemed to establish the metaphoric resonance of the landscape his characters occupied as being open to interpretation through that frame of existential absurdity that had marked his emergence, but also through a concept not of the 'human condition', but of human rights. The scrutiny of slippery language and dialogic interactions between characters in Pinterland had begun to shift focus not only onto the interaction among humans, and classes, and genders, but also onto the public languages of power. The examination of the ability to exclude from the room had shifted from friend to lover to family member, from imaging a sense of exile from Sidcup to confronting the possible genocidal dismissal of an entire group. And in this period the international acknowledgement of the resonance of these metaphors grew and developed until the awarding to Pinter of the Nobel Prize for literature in 2005 seemed to illustrate for the world's media that this was work of great and lasting human import, not the rantings of a paranoid fantasist.

In 1996 a group of Kurdish men, including a 12-year-old boy, were arrested, held, and interrogated by armed police in north London. Their crime was to have taken part in a rehearsal of *Mountain Language* in a community hall. The context, and the nature of the imprisonment, is an ironic, and bathetic, comparison with the world of Turkish government repression or Latin American dictatorship. The detention lasted five hours; was condemned by a judge as an 'extraordinary state of affairs'; and resulted, four years later, in London's Metropolitan Police Service paying the men £55,000 in compensation in an out-of-court settlement. The group were émigré Kurds, rehearsing at the Kurdistan Workers' Association in Stoke Newington, north London, not far from Pinter's childhood home in Clapton. Dressed in combat fatigues and carrying fake guns – props borrowed from the National Theatre – they had been swooped upon by armed police after a report from a member of the public of fatigue-clad men holding hostages at gunpoint. In a scene the irony of which might provide ammunition to those who saw Pinter's UK context as a humane and freedom-loving antidote to the regimes he condemned, the men were held in a police van and forbidden to speak in their own language.[20] As the group's solicitor was quoted as saying at the case's outcome, 'if it weren't so serious it would be funny'.[21]

In 2007 the Free Theatre of Belarus, a celebrated dissident theatre company based in Minsk, performed extracts from *One for the Road* and *Mountain Language* as part of their first performance in the UK. Their director, Vladimir Scherban, described the plays as a 'bullseye into Byelorussian reality'.[22] Pinter's late 'political' works resonated internationally and with the moment, making clear that the abstractions of art can mesh provocatively in the shaming of political leaders and their followers and provide a beacon in darkness, their metaphors chiming with all abuses of power, and with all oppressions. It is in *Party Time* that Pinter produces his most direct analysis of the soft language and rituals of power within which such oppressive weight is clothed.

Notes

1   H. Pinter, *Party Time* (1991) in *Harold Pinter: Plays 4* (London: Faber, 2011), pp. 279–314 (p. 288).

2   There is a compelling account of the complexity of this argument in Christopher Bigsby's biography of Miller: C. Bigsby, *Arthur Miller, 1962–2005* (London: Weidenfeld and Nicolson, 2011), pp. 345–7.

3   H. Pinter, 'Arthur Miller's Socks', www.haroldpinter.org/politics/politics_torture.shtml (accessed 30 October 2015).

4   Pinter, *Party Time*, p. 284.

5   I. Wardle, *Independent on Sunday*, 10 November 1991, p. 23, quoted in M. Page, *File on Pinter* (London: Methuen, 1993), p. 89.

6   H. Pinter, 'Introduction' (1970) in *Harold Pinter: Plays 3* (London: Faber, 1996), p. 8.

7   H. Pinter, 'Writing for the Theatre' (1962) in *Pinter: Plays One* (London: Methuen, 1976), p. 10.

8   'A Play and its Politics: A Conversation between Harold Pinter and Nick Hern', in H. Pinter, *One for the Road* (London: Methuen, 1985), pp. 5–23.

9   M. Billington, 'Harold Pinter: Obituary', *Guardian*, 27 December 2008.

10 Amnesty International, *Chile: An International Report* (London: Amnesty International Publications, 1974).

11 J. Verdenius and K. Mastenbroek, *A Dirty Game, TV documentary* (Electrical Films, 2002).

12 Pinter, *One for the Road* (1984), in *Plays 4*, pp. 221–47 (p. 247).

13 A. Beckett, *Pinochet in Piccadilly* (London: Faber, 2002), p. 143.

14 H. Pinter, *Mountain Language* (1988), in *Plays 4*, pp. 249–78 (p. 262).

15 Ibid., p. 264.

16 D. Milne, 'Pinter's Sexual Politics' in P. Raby, *The Cambridge Companion to Harold Pinter* (Cambridge: Cambridge University Press, 2012), pp. 233–48 (p. 235).

17 "[Pinter's] plays about political interrogation and torture in prisons now appear prophetic in their envisioning of the systematic violence known to have been practiced in Guantanamo Bay, Abu Ghraib and similar political prisons where human rights have

been routinely violated in the name of democracy." R. Gordon, *Harold Pinter: The Theatre of Power* (Ann Arbor, MI: University of Michigan Press, 2012), p. 162.

18 See C. Brown, 'April 29th' in *The Lost Diaries* (London: Fourth Estate, 2019), pp. 137–8 for a particularly brilliant example, in which Pinter takes his meter reader for an agent of the state come to crush his dissident status.

19 C. Brown, 'The Lost Diaries', *Guardian*, 2 October 2010, www.theguardian.com/books/2010/oct/02/craig-brown-lost-diaries-parody (accessed 5 November 2015).

20 J. Hartley-Brewer, 'Met Pays Damages for Raid on Actors', *Guardian*, 3 February 2000, www.theguardian.com/uk/2000/feb/03/ukguns.juliahartleybrewer (accessed 5 November 2015).

21 Two accounts of this incident – a newspaper report by Duncan Campbell for the *Guardian* and the letter written by Pinter in the aftermath to the same paper – can be found in H. Pinter, *Various Voices: Prose, Poetry, Politics 1994–1998* (London: Faber, 1998), pp. 194–6.

22 A. Hickling, 'Being Harold Pinter', *Guardian*, 16 April 2007, www.theguardian.com/stage/2007/apr/16/theatre (accessed 5 November 2015).

2

Party Time

Party Time begins with two men, Terry and Gavin, caught in mid conversation at a party. Around them people talk, music plays, a waiter holds a tray of drinks. Two doors lead from the room. The younger man, Terry, is describing the rich luxury of a private members' club, its class, the tennis and swimming available, the complimentary drinks, the hot towels. The older, Gavin, is half-listening, and the mention of hot towels leads him into reflection about the rituals of the barbershops of his youth. The younger man seems to be out to impress the older with the glories of this club. The older man seems more detached, partially anchored by the conversation, but more interested in his own reflections than in the substance of what is being said to him. As Terry continues to describe the club's exclusive luxury, his connoisseur's tone is momentarily undermined by a jarring drop into a colloquial obscenity, thrown in as if it reinforces his argument.

We seem to be in the chilly territorial environment of earlier Pinter, of a range of plays in which the gathering and the room are spaces for figures to battle and barter over, and in which a single remark can include or exclude, definitively. As is the case in those earlier plays, this is a space of aspiration. The towels described are the empty tokens of luxury familiar from the 'afromosia tweed veneer' of Mick's pretend dream world in *The Caretaker*.[1] It is a male world, again, with two subtly competing figures, one holding power over the other. In *The Caretaker* the competition between the protagonists is revealed to be a matter of possession and loyalty. In *No Man's Land* it's a matter of ownership and dependence, of private spaces and personal survival. In *Party Time* the enigma of the opening suggests perhaps that we're in a world of corporate relations, of the power exchanges between senior and junior staff. Terry is the young apprentice, out to impress, the car salesman seeking a deal. In fact, as the scene progresses, it becomes clear that this opening exchange *is* a pitch, of sorts. Terry is recruiting Gavin, and in doing so requesting his patronage, cajoling and flattering: flattery that diminishes the flatterer even as it's given.

A woman, Dusty, enters, asking a question: 'Did you hear what's happened to Jimmy?'. It's not clear whom she's addressing or how she is connected to the two men. Terry answers her with a silencing mix of menace and bonhomie: 'Nobody's discussing it, sweetie. Do you follow me? Nothing's happened to Jimmy.' Terry appears to be intimate with Dusty, and his dismissal of Dusty's question is an order, not an answer. Whatever has happened to Jimmy may be urgent, and current, but it's a question that is not askable in this setting. The 'sweetie' belittles Dusty and that claim to control her is furthered in Terry's next line, a leering threat to 'spank' her. The tone of sexualised violence, of its threat and its use to intimidate, is to return, echoing through the relations between apparently powerful males and apparently subordinated females throughout, as it does in Pinter's other political plays. Dusty does not address

Terry's rebuke directly, but she continues to ask questions. Terry changes the subject, suggesting that Dusty tell Gavin about the club. In a disconcerting shift, Dusty's urgent dissent morphs into an enthusiastic endorsement of the club and its wonderful qualities – the beauty, the lighting, the pool. It is as if the morality of the moment is overridden by the situation's demand that she conform, obey, please. Dusty and Terry now chorus about the pool, and the pleasures it offers, until the appearance of another guest, Melissa, a woman of a similar age to Gavin.

Melissa's entrance brings direct reference to the world outside, and the situation in which the party is taking place: 'There's nobody on the streets, there's not a soul in sight, apart from some . . . soldiers.' We begin to see how the people in the room stand in relation to those events in the streets, and what links their competitive concern for luxury and security with what is happening in that outside world. Gavin's response is a combination of the reassuring and the dismissive: 'Oh, there's just been a little . . . you know . . .'. Terry breaks in, and introduces the two figures to each other. The new guest has a title, Dame Melissa. Gavin greets her, indicating for the first time that he is the host. Terry secures Melissa a glass of wine from a waiter, ignoring her reply when he asks what she'd like to drink. The two men are quickly allying to close off the moment of unease that Melissa's entrance has created, a female character's questions again disturbing the equilibrium of the party. At first, Dusty follows up the opportunity that Melissa's remarks have created, and it seems that there is a space for the discussion of events outside to break through Gavin and Terry's control of the social surface of the evening. However, the chance of solidarity between the two questioning women disappears as Melissa ignores Dusty and addresses Gavin with a pleasantry. Melissa's concern with the disruption in the streets is clearly of a different nature from Dusty's. For Melissa it seems only to be an inconvenience. She knows what to think and when to think it. This leaves Terry to home in once more on Dusty's disturbance of party etiquette. His response to her is again sharp, and this time stronger in its verbal aggression: 'all you have to do is shut up and enjoy the hospitality and mind your own fucking business'.

The opening of the play establishes that sense of a heightened, shifting, poetic realism that defines the 'Pinteresque'. In it the character structures and dialogues of a realist register are dislocated by switches in tone and logic; by nagging repetition of words and rhythms; by statements and actions, undermining the consistency of conventional character presentation. We seem to be able to draw conclusions about figures only for their own words to contradict them. A partial portrait of their standing, or their background, or their obsessions and attitudes is supplied, but it becomes clear that the focus is on the performative utterance of that language – on meaning being constructed in the moment of confrontation with others. Our search for the elements of a coherent story might be frustrated, but we can grasp the resonance of forms of speech and behaviour, and take the tone of the gathering. These are characters in the way that a Bacon or Auerbach painting is a portrait – fragments of a figure being focused on, worked at, and presented, with the effect of viewing human behaviour as through a haze of memory and impression. In this case we have an image of an elite, gathered in circumstances that they seem to have constructed but the full knowledge of which is shared only through patronage and favour. This is the world Irving Wardle recognised in the play, and we glimpse it in moments.

The next two sections of the play focus on other guests, and the tone of distanced, separated lives, presented as though in vitrines, foregrounds an emerging sense of the text as a display of the language and manners of an elite. Two women, Liz and Charlotte, sit on a sofa. They talk about a man, or rather Charlotte interjects as Liz speaks of a beautiful man she desired, and whom she saw another woman seduce at a party (possibly this one). The beauty she describes, of the man's mouth, eyes, and hands, gives way to a statement of the intensity of her desire ('I would have killed') and of her hatred for the woman who took him, the images growing more intense and surreal. The overstated incongruity continues as Charlotte's rejoinders become a kind of deadpan counselling, reflecting Liz's anger back to her. As we shall see, Charlotte's role throughout the play involves the ambiguous provocation of the excesses of those around her. If Terry is the constant voice of frantic control, resorting to violence when articulacy dries up, Charlotte is the subtle puller of rugs from under the feet of those with whom she is speaking. Like Dusty, Charlotte is of this party, dependent on it and conforming with it, but at a distance. She represents the nagging voice of dissent in the room.

The tone of intense overstatement, like a kind of adolescent ego-rage, drawn from Liz, also feeds the next exchange, between two men at the party. The lights come up on Fred and Douglas. Fred is holding forth about the state of the nation: 'We've got to make it work.' Douglas concurs: 'All this fucking about has to stop.' 'A bit of that', says Fred, clenching his fist. Douglas mirrors the action and repeats the phrase. And then he asks Douglas 'How's it going tonight?', and the unspoken nature of the actions on the street become clearer, along with Douglas' role in them. 'Like clockwork', Douglas replies, an apparent agent in the night's events. He then takes the opportunity of Fred's approval to outline his thinking, a political speech that starts strongly and then begins to fall into empty repetition. This is a familiar Pinter moment, the woozy line being walked by the proselytist of certainty, a moment that shares characteristics with the words of Goldberg in *The Birthday Party*, another figure of male authority beginning to crumble as he wanders into a forest of words.[2]

Douglas clenches his fist again, for emphasis. Fred tells him, 'You know, I really admire people like you.' Douglas' response, 'so do I', dislocates and disturbs the moment. It may be comic, a deliberate joke attaching to Fred's remark, or it may, as throughout when Pinter's sense of the absurd focuses on the poetic estrangement of language, frustrate the reading of the moment as literal and draw attention to the politics of the play as emblematic rather than specific. These twin interludes confirm the corruption of language and desire in the room, the romantic and the violent tied together with the idealising of strength and aggression.

The play shifts back to the previous group. Melissa, Dusty, Terry, and Gavin are talking about how well Melissa looks, Terry claiming that he has known her for a long time and that she always looks the same. Melissa puts her good health down to her membership of a new club; Terry says they were just telling Gavin all about it, and she and Gavin discuss the sports they play before she abruptly asks him what he does – a question that seems to open that space of uneasy challenge, and the threatened loss of power familiar across Pinter's work. Gavin replies enigmatically and Terry instantly leaps in to try and lighten the moment. From here the conversation continues in a collision of logic and shifting positions. An awkward discussion of boats and their pleasures follows, in which

Terry again seems to overreach himself as he tries to head off Dusty's involvement in the conversation. In response Dusty reopens the issue underlying the evening:

Does anyone know what's happened to my brother Jimmy?

The single word 'brother' echoes through the play from this point, placing the uncertainties of Dusty's previous questions and their dismissals in a new light. Terry's response is chill, direct, and cuts across Dusty's question, addressing the other guests. Terry reminds them he had made it clear to Dusty that discussion of what has happened to Jimmy is 'not on anyone's agenda'. Dusty replies defiantly: 'it's on my agenda'. Terry's response raises the temperature of the exchange, and suggests that anger is again disrupting his ability to present the necessary tone, or effectively to close down a dissenting voice. His loss of verbal fluency is in pointed contrast to Gavin's controlled observation: 'So odd, the number of men who can't control their wives.' Having issued this put-down, Gavin ignores Terry and continues a conversation with Melissa. Terry interjects, but there is no response. Instead, Gavin changes the subject, describing a walk in the woods he had taken, and remarking on his surprise at the number of squirrels that can still be found. This is another sounding of the note of insistent emotional nostalgia that enters the language of the group – in particular that of Gavin and Melissa – and that returns throughout the play. It is a romanticised echoing of former ages and attitudes, caught in wistful recollection. The conversation continues across the desperate Terry as Melissa recalls her own childhood memories of wildlife: of hawks, particularly 'the kestrel. The way it flew, and hovered, over my valley . . . . It made me cry. I still cry.' Memory, as so often in Pinter, here becomes a device to project into the present, shaped and narrated according to the requirements of the power games of the moment. Melissa's evoking of the kestrel also brings into play a resonant image of haughty, fascistic power, the projected fantasy of such power hanging above the throng of the ordinary, ready to strike.

The play switches back to the other guests. Fred is introduced by Liz to Charlotte. They know each other, to Liz's surprise. 'He gave me a leg up in life', says Charlotte, a remark that Douglas leaps on: 'was it exciting?'. Charlotte responds, challenging the innuendo: 'Oh yes, I'm still trembling.' It is an ambiguous exchange that can be seen either to indulge or to confront Douglas. Charlotte's directness seems to stop Douglas in his tracks for a moment. Liz interrupts to draw attention back to the surface of the event, in a gushing speech about the tastefulness of the party, and the importance of maintaining such qualities in a decaying world.

Liz's words don't deflect the attention from Fred and Charlotte's past acquaintance, but the enigma of Charlotte's role – as challenger or as confederate – remains, with Fred mentioning that Charlotte was married, although he can't recall to whom. His remark is followed by the stage direction 'silence', an indication of a hefty shift of weight in Pinter's dramatic landscapes. 'He died', Charlotte replies. Fred's memory seems strategic, of a piece with this territory of shifting loyalties and dangers, of the gathering of figures whose influence, or presence, or existence is liable to slide out of view at any moment. Charlotte now seems clearly aligned with Dusty as a dissenting voice. For Dusty the figure about whom she cannot ask questions is her brother. For Charlotte it is her husband, although at this point we are still unsure of his significance to her – a figure from the past, perhaps disowned, but perhaps still to be avenged.

Douglas now takes the lead in this competitive exercise in improvisation to try and restore equilibrium and to find some common ground. His rhapsody is about another form of escape, as he invites the guests to summer on their island. It is an escape into nature, and into the wildness of a sirocco-swirled landscape, an idyllic place, barely populated. Douglas describes the island as the kind of setting in which one can contemplate the sunset and feel nearer to one's Maker. It is a picture of a Spartan place of origin, albeit one that is serviced by the local population for this elite's convenience, and it forms part of the bedrock of normality at this party, an Edenic return, like the valleys and barbershops of youth, or the exclusive club of the party's present. Whether it is myth or 'reality' is, as with so much of the world of the play, irrelevant. It is enough for the figures in the room that it is invoked.

The scene shifts back to Terry and Dusty, engaged in a furious, switchback battle of intimacy and hatred. Terry is asking Dusty if she realises who Gavin is, but Dusty seems unconcerned. She praises Gavin's courtesy, a dying form of manners: 'He'll send me flowers in the morning', she says. Terry's response is a typically blunt, exasperated put-down: 'No he bloody won't.' Dusty responds by asking Terry if she's failed him, taunting him now, wondering whether she will become a victim of Terry's lust for vengeance once they get home. The stakes raised, Terry indulges his contempt for his wife with relish, aligning her with the opposition and unleashing an angry and macabre fantasy of their destruction. It is a vision of the possibilities that absolute power gives and culminates in Terry's evocation of an image of the poisoning of mothers' milk so that 'every baby would drop dead before it opened its perverted bloody mouth'.

The characterisation of the mouth, the source of dissent, as the place where all of Terry's threatened violence is aimed, broadens the play's concern with the power of utterance. The denial of the ability to announce and coalesce dissent makes the closed, silenced mouth of the infant the image of a total triumph of power. Yet it is the inability of such torrents of violent speech to silence those voices that ask troubling questions at the party that drives the angry frustration of the figures. Somehow they find themselves unable to realise fully their desire for control. Dusty continues to resist and to raise the stakes of the argument, finally silencing Terry with a casual return to her insistent question, 'Oh incidentally, what's happened to Jimmy?'.

The action shifts to a dialogue between Fred and Charlotte, a contrasting minefield of short call-and-answer exchanges. Fred asks Charlotte how her husband died. She replies that it was a short illness. Fred suggests that was for the best. Charlotte disputes this, and then adds, almost as an afterthought, and in an echo of Dusty, the chilling:

CHARLOTTE: Oh by the way, he wasn't ill.

It is a characteristic Pinteresque non sequitur, opening a gap between what has happened and what is being said about it. Fred changes the subject to Charlotte's beauty. She persists in her dissent, asking what is happening in the street. Fred deflects her enquiry, suggesting that this can be left to the men of the party.

In the style of his previous homily, Douglas begins to reminisce about his early married life with Liz, a eulogy concerning the perfect past in which he worked hard for his family, imaged in a nostalgic word-picture. A tone of self-justification against an imagined opponent enters the dialogue as he details the heroism of his ordinary striving. Here there is no avoiding the play's direct engagement with a rhetoric of family, respectability, and aspiration that is contemporaneous with the play's emergence, part of its satiric take on the self-articulation of the Conservative administration under Prime Minister Margaret Thatcher in the UK in the late 1980s and early 1990s. Melissa's partial impersonation of Thatcher is another echo, as are Douglas' and Fred's commonplaces about strength and order. This suggestion that there is a parallel between the nightmares of this party and the attitudes of the 1990s Tory administration might seem to support the characterisation of Pinter's vision of 1990s Britain as paranoid, his involvement with the 20 June Group a form of fashionable martyrdom through which the British Left fantasised itself to be living under the totalitarianism of the Eastern Bloc or the military dictatorships of Latin America. Yet the play is careful to step away from such direct alignments, to employ them only as echoes and traces. In this respect its anatomisation of those party to the Party has a wider frame of resonance. In the period after the fall of the Berlin Wall, in a South Africa experiencing the end of Apartheid, in an early 1990s recognition that authoritarian regimes could find themselves under threat from the force of popular unrest, the play examines the ways in which an elite might create an imaginary for itself, one that slips away even in the moments it is being constructed. *Party Time* focuses on the self-protective rhetoric of entitlement, the empty absurdism of the language of political strength. The core of the play, in exchanges between characters that celebrate strength and romanticise violence, suggests

it is presenting a critique of right-wing power.[3] In the literature and actions of Fascism the fantasy of the performative
moment of transcendence returns repeatedly as a motif – a
longed-for ideal transformation of everything debased and
fallen in a triumphant rapture of the righteous, and *Party
Time*'s characters ooze righteousness. Douglas is presented
throughout as the reiterator of such ideals, and concludes his
monologue by kissing the ever compliant Liz on the cheek.

At this moment the room darkens and the light from the
other, so far unused, door grows stronger. The lights then
rise on the whole company being addressed by Terry, who
is back on his favourite topic, the club. This time the club is
metamorphosing into the epitome of all things ideal, a perfect
space of a kind of malign *communitas*, though a *communitas*
based on vague qualities – ones that seem to fade whenever
Terry tries to render them concrete. His undermining of his
own attempts to sell the club's message, revealed in his fatal
lack of sophistication, are captured in scrabbling attempts to
describe its atmosphere of deference and service along with
a bathetic emphasis on its value for money. Somehow Terry
never seems secure in his membership of either literal, or
metaphorical, clubs.

London is a city of clubs. The centre of the city has its
superclubs and tourist-focused cabarets, but it also houses a
host of private members' clubs, of social, trade and political associations, of sports and welfare organisations, their
structures built on mutual interest, their rituals, codes and
habits rooted in the shared values of their members. These are
gathering spaces that define their members by common pur-
pose or value, that create a norm of activity and identity. They
act as a focal point for a community and its values, and offer
the opportunity to circulate and network with like-minded

people. The centre of the city offers a range of buildings that house these kinds of associations. Pinter himself had 'clubbable' aspects. He was a member of the Marylebone Cricket Club, and as an established figure in the arts he was patron and chair of the Gaieties Cricket Club. The rituals and associations of these organisations create structures, hierarchies, affiliations, loyalties. That Pinter is ready to anatomise such organisations, which were both his natural milieu and the constituents of power and exclusion that he despised, suggests that the image of the lives under scrutiny captured in *Party Time* is more than a simple condemnation of power and its ways of operating. We are all caught up in and exploiters of networks of patronage and preferment, just as we are all exclusive and all ready to police the boundaries of what we find acceptable, to control the entry and exit from that room of which Pinter is such a persistent explorer. And we are also the generous participants in networks of charity and support, of invitation and recognition, of inclusion and solidarity. The essence of such associations is in part registered in the buildings, the trappings, the shared values expressed in the association, the performative rituals that Pinter's drama so focuses on – whether it be in examining the relationships among families, siblings, lovers, friends or associates, comrades, co-conspirators. And in part such associations are also things of language, of the literal expression of agreement and coincidence. This language world is not a fixed space of confluence and commitment but a shifting territory constructed in performance, and when Melissa now addresses the guests with an enthusiastic eulogy for the clubs and friends of her youth a sudden collapse into incoherence illustrates this slippery relation between language and meaning.

The collapse comes in a moment in which Melissa is recall-ing the friends who populated the clubs of her youth, and then finds herself brought up short by the realisation of their loss – clubs and friends alike. This tips her from a conventional description of the past as a rootstock for her values into a contemplation of the double-edged nature of memory, with its readiness to comfort tight-bound to its potential to disturb. Her rhetoric switches from a routine of public pronounce-ment to a slow decay into horrified self-recognition. Across Pinter's work figures share moments akin to this, moments of what might be called 'hollowness', when they recognise that the business of their lives may be conducted on uncertain ground. In Pinter's plays such insights are often aligned with the familiar existential concerns of his absurdist peers, with acts of speech and events that build a platform of activity and assertion as distractions from the cold reality of experience. Yet in this phase of Pinter's career, what happens next indicates a shift in his aesthetic. Perhaps Melissa's crumbling is a cracking of the composed surface under recognition of the fragility of life. Certainly the silence that follows it indicates something of this quality. However, her recovery is equally performative – a resurrection of the spirit of conformity and, from Pinter, a satiric jibe at the fascination with renewal among an elite for whom survival of status is all that matters. The clubs perished, Melissa declares, because of their lack of values, and she begins to recognise the significance of this even as she speaks, with a ringing declaration of the importance of their new club, founded as it is (though it clearly isn't) on 'a moral awareness, a set of moral values which is – I have to say – unshakeable, rigorous, fundamental, constant.'

Gavin approves Melissa's words as the other guests chime in with their agreement. Gavin uses the moment to praise the party, speaking 'as a very happy host' and asking to join the club, to which Terry responds by electing him as an honorary member. As laughter and applause die away Gavin raises the topic of what has caused the disruption encountered by the guests on their way to the party. He offers his apologies, clearly not only the host of the party but also the instigator of the events to which he has euphemistically referred, confessing that 'between ourselves we've had a bit of a round-up this evening', and that order is now restored. The tensions of the evening seem to have been skirted, the ensemble is drawn back together. The language of service, of party, of normality and order meshes together in Gavin's address and his gracious thanks to his guests.

The stage now darkens. The partygoers are caught in silhouette and the light from a door off 'intensifies, burning into the room'. From this door another figure enters, not a guest at the party, but a presence that the party has never quite been able to forget. He stands at the door, 'thinly dressed'.

> Sometimes I hear things. Then it's quiet.
>
> I had a name. It was Jimmy. People called me Jimmy. That was my name.

He sits in the dark, listening, hearing his heartbeat. He describes terrible noises that come unbidden, and that scramble his other senses. Afterwards, when it is quiet, he still hears a heartbeat, but now he speaks of how it might be someone else's. Identity is lost. This figure is dispossessed, no longer capable of action, only able to listen: ' I sit sucking the dark.' The jolting image is repeated. The sum of Jimmy's dispossession, isolation, and terror: 'The dark is in my mouth and I suck it. It's the only thing I have. It's mine. It's my own. I suck it.' The 'suck' is a shocking, ugly image, a poetic enjambment that breaks the rhythm of the scene. It also enforces the sense of a breakdown of primary relations, the suck of nourishment or pleasure here replaced by a latching on to a void.

There is no information that locates Jimmy in time or space, other than the suggestion that he is in some sort of prison, in proximity to some sort of horror afflicting others. He doesn't describe his own interrogation or torture. He is a witness to the torture of others, by that proximity, through sound, and a witness who becomes indistinguishable from the victims, in the darkness.

Jimmy's presence is of a piece with the appearance of victims in each of the plays of this period of Pinter's work. In *One for the Road* we are with the interrogator and the interrogatees, though the threatened violence mostly remains off stage and we only see its aftermath. In *Mountain Language* we watch the victims forced to respond to their captors. In the short play *The New World Order*, the premiere of which preceded *Party Time* by a matter of months, the interrogatee is also placed centre stage, a silent, blindfolded figure who is at the mercy of the double act of menace and threat carried out by Des and Lionel – the reduced versions of Goldberg and McCann of yesteryear.[4] Here Jimmy's appearance focuses attention on the absence of the imprisoned figure from the language of the party. The euphemisms and jokes of the partygoers mask the existence of such a figure, reduced, removed, hidden. For the partygoers, the events on the streets have been an inconvenience, or a reminder of the tenuous grip they hold on the security offered by invitation to the party and the club. But Jimmy is one of those who have been rounded up, and his fate now is to be beyond language. The drama brings him into presence, and lets him speak back to power in a moment that answers the question Dusty has so persistently asked.

Notes

1 H. Pinter, *The Caretaker* (1960), in *Collected Plays: Two* (London: Faber, 1996), pp. 1–76 (p. 58).

2 Goldberg's attempt to state what he believes in the face of McCann's apparent unease at the need to go up 'again' to Stanley ends in the repetition of the unfinished statement 'because I believe that the world is . . .' in tones respectively described in Pinter's stage directions as 'vacant', 'desperate', and 'lost'. H. Pinter, *The Birthday Party* (1957) in *Collected Plays: One* (London: Faber, 1996), pp. 1–81 (p. 72).

3 Basil Chiasson examines the particularity of Pinter's use of language in these plays as a skewering of Neo-Liberal discourse; B. Chiasson, 'Pinter's Political Dramas: Staging Neo-Liberal Discourse and Authoritarianism' in M. Taylor-Batty, *The Theatre of Harold Pinter* (London: Bloomsbury Methuen, 2014), pp. 249–66.

4 H. Pinter, *The New World Order* (1991), in *Plays 4*, pp. 269–78.

3

Wentworth days

The Wentworth Estate in Surrey, west of London, is a prime piece of London stockbroker belt (or perhaps we might call it oligarch belt, the social soup of London being rapidly thinned by the rising house prices of the past decade to the point where the places once occupied by the merchants are now probably only occupied by the mega-rich). Wentworth houses an international golf course, a range of tennis clubs and sports grounds, and a sweep of mansions. It sits beside the Bourne River, just as the river enters the expanse of Virginia Water on the edge of Windsor Great Park. Covering 2.5 kilometres and home to a little under 2,000 people in a mixture of mansions, village, and both private and public roads, it is one of London's 'premier' estates, with its five- and six-bedroomed detached mansions currently on the market at between £8 million and £11 million. At the point of her retirement in 1990 Margaret Thatcher moved into a five-bedroomed house on a more modest private estate next to a golf course in the prosperous village of Dulwich in south London. She reputedly never lived in the gated development, but Wentworth, its 1920s houses and their modern copies built on a grander scale, is a model of the dream of secluded escape that Thatcher's house aped. Harold Pinter's own London residence, in a very expensive area of Holland Park, indicated quite how immersed in a world of privilege Pinter remained even after the Regents Park era, which gave rise to *Old Times* and *No Man's Land*, and the apparent contradictions of such contexts provided some of the ammunition for the kind of satirical jibes at left-wing luvvies or Hampstead socialists that were aimed at Pinter and his 20 June associates. Yet it also meant that the world of exclusivity behind gated driveways was a world that might be mined for its details and habits, for how it might be to see and hear the elite act and speak for themselves.

At school in the early 1980s I listened to the radio broadcast of the parliamentary debate concerning Britain's decision to go to war with Argentina over the invasion of the Falkland Islands in 1982 (a debate mirrored as I write in the impassioned parliamentary tussles over whether or not the UK should join the bombing of ISIL in Syria). There was no question in my mind that this was a war Britain should not fight. Pacifist principle told me so, and, as the conflict led on to serious casualties in the British army and navy I felt increasingly certain, most particularly when the sinking of the Argentinian battleship the *General Belgrano*, proven to have been torpedoed by a British submarine while apparently sailing away from the total exclusion zone declared around the islands by Britain, led to the deaths of 323 Argentinian sailors.[1] The campaign ended in the surrender of the Argentine forces, and the debate over the rightful ownership of the land continues in heated – and sometimes rather farcical[2] – circumstances today.

I find my youthful certainty difficult to support now. I admire its blithe assurance about principle, and I remain

convinced that this was not a territory whose ownership should have been decided by violence – the history of
Britain's colonial withdrawals suggests that compromise and
diplomacy are the only ways out of such an impasse. I find it
harder to understand my certainty in the face of the nature of
the Argentine junta. The military government that had taken
the Falklands was the descendant of the one that had staged
the 1976 coup and 'disappeared' up to 30,000 of its citizens.
Same uniforms, different faces. As I write, the *Times* newspaper
is carrying a story about the discovery by the Grandmothers
of the Plaza de Mayo of the 118th child kidnapped by the
junta during this period, the legacy of the military government and its 'national reorganisation process' still looming
over the country.[3] And whatever the controversial figure of
Margaret Thatcher stood guilty of through her time in office,
she retained a glimmer of humanity, didn't she? She may have
veered close to, her husband may have expressed views akin
to, she may have allowed into her party figures with views
not far from fascism, but she wasn't, was she, a fascist? This
was the label used by the parody student protestor of that era,
Rik, in the BBC television sitcom *The Young Ones* – a caricature of overstated political naivety – and exaggeration of their
own oppression was the kind of accusation often aimed at the
radical British Left of the time. The Conservative administration was not, despite the excesses of the miner's strike or the
conflict in Northern Ireland, a dictatorship, nor did it oper-
ate a totalitarian state. Yet the figures against whom Margaret
Thatcher sent British forces, those whose nationalistic military adventure the invasion of the Falklands had been, were
just this, and their attack was a last desperate bid to hold their
authority in place.[4] Four months after deposing the previous
leader of the junta, General Leopold Galtieri had reversed his

growing domestic unpopularity by launching the invasion of the Malvinas, as the islands are known to Argentine nationalists. By the end of the conflict Galtieri was deposed and the path toward democracy (along with the General's own indictment for crimes committed during the Dirty War) opened. The battle to liberate the Falkland Islands became a battle that also liberated the Argentine nation. Ironically, it seems as though Thatcher's Task Force had struck a blow for democracy and freedom that resonated further than the Falklands.

Except things get even more complicated when considered from this perspective. They are complicated by the militant nationalist rhetoric surrounding ownership of the islands from recent, democratically elected Argentine governments – nationalism is not the preserve of dictators. And they are complicated by the fact that a key ally of the UK in the Falklands campaign, one whose lending of military bases and the right of overflight for British aircraft made missions against mainland targets in Argentina possible for the Task Force, was General Augusto Pinochet Duarte, then still President, by a dictatorially managed plebiscite, of neighbouring Chile – the same Pinochet whose 1973 coup ushered in a dark age of repression, torture, and murderous disappearances that anticipated, overlapped with, and encouraged the abuses of the Argentine generals. There had been cooperation and collaboration between the two countries' dictatorships when the battle was against 'subversion'. That had now reverted to the bad blood that made them historically tense neighbours. Argentinian novelist Jorge Luis Borges famously characterised the battle between Argentina and the UK over the Falklands as 'two bald men, fighting over a comb'.[5] Perhaps Pinochet made that three.

Though when Margaret Thatcher went to visit him and to take tea at his house on the Wentworth Estate in 1999, baldness wasn't a concern for either party. Then Pinochet was dapper, neat, well coiffed and wealthy, even if he appeared a little dazed and tired. The Thatcher hairstyle was familiarly magnificent and solid on her head. The picture taken at the time of the couple and Pinochet's wife Lucia in front of the grand entrance of the rented mansion captures old friends conducting old friends' business with ease, in seclusion. Now Thatcher is the supportive ally, presenting herself in her associate's hour of need. She has arrived to lend succour to an old man who finds himself under house arrest in a country far from home, outrageously traduced by a third party. Arrested by the UK government at the request of a Spanish magistrate, the ex-dictator was at bay in Surrey. He waited there while the extraordinary matter of his requested extradition to stand trial accused of crimes committed against Spanish citizens was adjudicated on by the Law Lords, the highest legal authority in the UK. Thatcher's support appeared to condemn the British government's cooperation with Spain and to suggest that by all natural codes of justice this arrest could not be tolerated in a modern democracy.

Pinochet's incarceration at Wentworth came as a consequence of a long, slow, and hard-won battle for justice. Pinochet stepped down from the Presidency of Chile in 1990 after a lengthy transition to democratic elections largely created by international pressure. He remained Commander-in-Chief of the Chilean army for another decade, and was handed a permanent senatorial role and immunity from prosecution for any past actions under laws he had passed during the last months of his dictatorship. The transition to democracy gradually uncovered the true nature of his rule in a period during which the gradual dispersal of dictatorial regimes in South America and the campaigning of organisations like

the Plaza de Mayo Mothers in Argentina brought legal challenge against those military and political figures who, previously untouched, had acted with impunity. In Spain Judge
Balthazar Garzon[6] had concerned himself with the cases of
a number of Spanish citizens caught up in the aftermath of
the Chilean coup who had been murdered, who had suffered
torture, or who had disappeared. It was his issuing of a warrant for Pinochet's arrest through the principle of universal
jurisdiction in cases of crimes against humanity that led to
the General's being detained at the private London Clinic,
which he had entered for a routine operation while visiting
London on his annual holiday (during which he was also in
the habit of making a visit to Margaret Thatcher). The left-
leaning British government of Tony Blair's Labour Party had
been elected in a wave of popular support for liberal values
and tolerance and the wiping clean of compromise in the
application of moral principles in government. An 'ethical'
foreign policy had been promised, and stalwarts of activism
and human rights law were part of the Europe-friendly network of ministers and officials in the government. Faced with
the Spanish arrest warrant the Home Office had to act, and so
Jack Straw, the Home Secretary, ordered Pinochet's detention.

The arrest provoked outrage and joy in contrasting meas-
ure in Chile, but the official government line was that this was
an affront. Even were Pinochet to be found guilty of crimes
that had so far been unsuccessfully pursued in his home
country this was not how justice should proceed. Pinochet
should be tried by his countrypeople, not by an old colonial
power asserting an old colonial justice. The following months
saw a slow-motion political crisis unfold in both countries.
Margaret Thatcher's fiery, adamant self-righteousness took
her to Wentworth to deliver a message of support – one

she repeated some months later in a speech – her first to the Conservative Party Conference since her loss of power nine years previously – that could have come from the mouth of Pinter's Melissa. Its depiction of the agonies of unjust incarceration could not but appear as fiercely ironic:

> We know a good deal about the catalogue of abuses which occurred. We know that Senator Pinochet was treated on his arrival, as on previous occasions, as an honoured guest . . . . We know that he was arrested by night, on his bed of pain after a spinal operation, in circumstances which would do credit to a police state. We know that he was held first in a tiny room at a clinic under sedation, and then in a house where he wasn't even allowed to set foot in the garden.[7]

Thatcher's support for the Wentworth One was rendered incongruous both by its vehemence – her speech claims Pinochet both as the vital Falklands ally to whom Britain owes a huge debt, and as defender of democracy and economic liberalism against communism and Left subversion – and by the lack of other figures prepared to step forward in his support. One of those few was Norman Lamont, the former Chancellor of the Exchequer under Thatcher's successor as Prime Minister, John Major. Lamont became a vocal champion of Pinochet during his house arrest. Some years later Lamont stood (for some reason, in my mind's eye, in a striped blazer, although I suspect I have invented this for him), on Paddington Station platform in London. I stood near him, angry. Given the chance by our coincidental proximity I wanted to tell him how disgusted I was by his conduct, his support for a man whose regime was responsible for so much horror. Like Pinter, Lamont was not a figure who was obliged to become involved in Pinochet's case, whose diplomatic or political responsibilities required him to speak up about the correct management of such a situation. His commitment appears to have been a matter of conscience. But I didn't disrupt that particular party. This was, by then, a backbench MP who had moved quickly, a one-man loyalty campaign, to support the dictator, isolated in the suburbs of his ally's city. Lamont's defence of the General brought the Augusto Pinochet Foundation's award of a 'Star of Honour and Merit' for his 'extraordinary and valiant attitude in defending the honour of General Pinochet'[8]. At the award ceremony in Santiago, Lamont declared that 'it is easy and a mistake to judge yesterday by today's climate and today's standards'.

While Pinochet smiled for the cameras in Surrey, a forceful squad of lobbyists and counter-lobbyists battled for publicity in central London. Harold Pinter welcomed the decision to detain him in an article for the *Independent*:

> That Pinochet will be made to face his past is an uplift-ing prospect. At last, this man, irrespective of his pos-ition, is to be made answerable for his crimes. It is remarkable that, on the 50th anniversary of the United Nations' Universal Declaration of Human Rights, the British Government has taken a stand for those rights and for international law. We are only beginning to comprehend the consequences for the restoration of the faith of people everywhere in the system of inter-national justice. The world has recognised that the sys-tematic violation of human rights can be considered a crime against humanity.[9]

Pinter and Lamont represented the two sides of the battle over Pinochet, both figures of prominence and influence, one an implacable supporter of the man he saw as a symbol of independent sovereignty and the rule of law, the other an anatomiser of the platitudes and practices of the elite for whom disconnection rendered vicious excess possible. On the night of the initial denial of Pinochet's appeal, Pinter and Lamont were in the studios of BBC Television's *Newsnight* current affairs programme, and Pinter's wife, Lady Antonia Fraser, records Pinter's sense of triumphing in the debate: 'He looked calmly vengeful on screen and saw off Norman Lamont, who said that the Chilean people had given Pinochet immunity. Harold: "No, Pinochet gave Pinochet immunity."'[10] Lamont's support for Pinochet was also expressed as support for the idea of sovereignty and the right of self-determination for nation-states; 'for diplomacy to work, you need immunity from prosecution for heads of state'.[11] More widely, commentary in support of the General tended to place the focus on the necessity of the 1973 coup – the sense that the Left activism of the era across South America was both Soviet-sponsored, aimed at destabilising democratic government, and ruthlessly violent. For many commentators on the Right the 'dark age' of post-coup Chile was actually an Enlightenment of monetarism, the free-market buccaneering economic philosophy – driven by the 'Chicago Boys',[12] a group of American-educated economists in Pinochet's government – which became Thatcher's own hardline philosophy. That Pinochet's repression in fact made little distinction between those who aligned themselves with armed struggle and those who merely sought to dissent and proselytise for social change was an unfortunate accident of history from this perspective. The position represented by Pinter, that moral and ethical considerations outweigh the political, was also uncompromising and principled, and it was expressed both in public debate and through the exploration in drama of poetic metaphor – the 'abstracted realism' that Milne notes is Pinter's own term for his technique – which examined the language and concepts through which impunity could be maintained.

At this point the Pinochet case was at the forefront of international debate on the prosecution of crimes against humanity. In 1995 in The Hague the International Criminal Tribunal for the Former Yugoslavia heard its initial case, marking the first large-scale investigation of post-conflict crimes since Nuremburg. United Nations-sponsored tribunals were opening over Rwanda (1994) and, later, the Khmer Rouge rule in Cambodia (2003). In South Africa the Truth and Reconciliation Commission (1996) was in progress, seeking a mode of restorative justice that could address the violence of the past. Similarly, in the UK the Good Friday Agreement of 1998 was bringing the process of facing the legacy of past conflict, controversially, into the open. As Pinter declared in interview, while the House of Lords considered Pinochet's situation, he was:

> interested in the proper observance of international law, if there is such a thing, because pure revenge has no bounds, no structure . . .
>
> The central thing is recognition. People in places like Chile and Argentina and Uruguay and Brazil – the mothers of the disappeared – they want these crimes to be acknowledged. You don't have to string up old Pinochet. No, you say: 'Look, Pinochet, this is what you did. Basically you're a loathsome, vile mass murderer. Stand there and listen to this, then you can fuck off.'[13]

It was an ironic echo of the directness of language so characteristic of the play.

In his biography of Pinter, the English theatre critic Michael Billington notes the critique of *Party Time* that came from other writers after its opening. Discussing the words of Edward Bond, John McGrath, and John Arden, three leading figures in the politically committed British theatre since the 1960s, Billington writes of concerns that the play lacked a specific, concrete context. Suggesting that it evoked the style of the Spanish surrealist filmmaker Luis Buñuel, Billington outlines how the language of the gathering clearly signals that this is a satire of right-wing power but also makes the point that were the play to be read as a portrait of 'a set of champagne socialists delighting in a successful left-wing coup, Pinter's point would still be the same: that the myopic acceptance of suffering and repression in the name of order and stability is morally unforgivable'.[14] The text makes a direct anatomisation of the evasive management of power, and power that resides with the male figures of the play, focusing on the self-protective rhetoric of entitlement, the empty absurdism of the language of political strength. The core of the play, in exchanges between characters who celebrate strength and romanticise violence, suggests it is indeed presenting a critique of right-wing power, but Pinter's work is both specific and limited in its applicability. It examines the authoritarian abuse of power as that power seeks to denigrate difference, as it celebrates conformity and derides challenge, as it demands the triumph of an aggressively conservative spirit and as it asserts a masculine version of sexualised violence against terrorised and subjected women. That rape should have become a weapon of terror against civilian populations in the Bosnian conflict, and sexual reproduction a device for the reshaping of social dissent in the military dictatorships of Latin America, illustrates the moral power of Pinter's depiction of the terrorising figures of his authoritarians.

In the second edition of a study of Pinter written in 2002, Penelope Prentice looks across the 'strong' female characters of Pinter's work and at the ways in which various critics have sought to explore their supposed depth of empathy and imagination, qualities that the male figures in the plays tend to lack, or fail to express. She cites Michael Billington's referencing of Dusty as 'an agent of opposition' as an example of this attribution of distinctive qualities to women. While recognising that the female characters in Pinter's plays do indeed often offer a corrective to the male and stand as figures of resistance, Prentice questions whether this means that they have any significant agency, and singles out Dusty as a character whose role in *Party Time* can't be read as a straightforward image of female empowerment. Prentice suggests that Dusty's dissent derives not from some innately greater imaginative or empathetic power specific to women but from her close relation to Jimmy, and that, notwithstanding her position in relation to him and to the elite partygoers, she still 'has no power to save him'. For Prentice, this depiction by Pinter of women whose capacity even to imagine agency is limited by their oppression raises a question: 'Is Pinter subtly confronting these issues concerning half the population of the world, as some contemporary women writers are doing more explicitly, to awaken women as well as others who are oppressed to their own responsibility?'[15] In addressing this question Prentice compares Pinter's approach to those of other contemporary texts that examine oppression in order to expose it, or that offer what she considers a progressive pathway beyond it. In a similar vein Drew Milne suggests that the depiction of gendered oppression in Pinter's work may in fact reproduce the things it seeks to undermine, and notes that sometimes in his plays, 'greater dramatic resourcefulness is given to those who abuse power. The devil's party seems stronger and more compelling.'[16] Pinter's poetic images are not straightforwardly aligned.

This sense of ambiguity in positioning the 'attitude' of a text is furthered in Pinter's final play. Like *Party Time*, Pinter's *Ashes to Ashes* also animates the territories of power. First staged in 1996 it steps back from reference to contemporary circumstances to offer an enigmatic image of histories of power, oppression, and loss. The play dramatizes themes and subjects touched on throughout Pinter's career, but most explicitly draws the resonances of the other political plays into a network of memory and of haunting images of trauma.

Ashes to Ashes concerns a woman and a man: Rebecca and Devlin. Set in a house that at some point Rebecca tells us is in Dorset, the play begins with Devlin seemingly demanding Rebecca's subjugation. He is telling her to kiss his fist, and then to allow him to hold her by the throat. He does this as a prelude to quizzing her about her past, and apparently about her relationship with another man. Yet none of the elements of this past are established as consistent 'facts'. Memory circles round on itself, with Rebecca's words replaying events. Rebecca tells stories of watching a man and a child hurrying through the streets of a city, followed by a woman with a baby. She speaks of seeing crowds of prisoners being marched through the Dorset landscape and into the sea to drown, herself a helpless witness to massacre. She speaks of visiting a factory with her lover and seeing the uniformed workers act with total obedience in front of him, an obedience she took to be respect but that we read as fear. She recounts how in the whole factory she had been unable to find a bathroom. She then remembers watching her lover at a train station, marching along the platform as people gathered:

> And my best friend, the man I had given my heart to, the man I knew was the man for me the moment we met, my dear, my most precious companion, I watched him walk down the platform and tear all the babies from the arms of their screaming mothers.[17]

The figures in this play are haunted by the shapes of European history; by the breaking of horror into the world of ordered contentment; and by the complicity of those who looked without seeing, or who joined with the powerful, pursuing their own interests. Rebecca appears, like Dusty and Charlotte in *Party Time*, to have been intimate with power, and for that intimacy to have revealed the horror of power's abuses to her. Yet those moments of revelation seem to have shifted her complicity to an identification with the victimised, one that undermines the privileged isolation of parties and country houses, by separation from oppression, its mechanisms, and consequences. In the final scenes of the play Rebecca's mixture of security, complicity, submission, and resistance feeds into a speech in which her memories seem to coalesce into a single event. She recalls the woman following the man and child in the street, carrying a baby, and then she recalls carrying a baby herself, a baby hidden in a bundle, onto a platform among crowds of people, only for it to be taken from her. When the journey ended she met a woman she knew who asked after the child. Rebecca describes her reply: 'And I said what baby? I don't have a baby.'

In 2015, some twenty years after Pinter's final play was written, the 94-year-old Oskar Groening stood trial in Lüneburg, Germany, for his complicity in the Holocaust as an SS clerk overseeing the sorting of prisoners' possessions on their arrival at Auschwitz. In 2005 Matthias Geyer had interviewed Groening for the German newspaper *Der Spiegel*, an interview that captures the past actor in an atrocity caught in the web of memory:

> The man rests his right leg on a stool. He is very calm and speaks quietly – and tells the story of the man he once was.
>
> 'A new shipment had arrived. I had been assigned to ramp duty, and it was my job to guard the luggage. The Jews had already been taken away. The ground in front of me was littered with junk, left-over belongings. Suddenly I heard a baby crying. The child was lying on the ramp, wrapped in rags. A mother had left it behind, perhaps because she knew that women with infants were sent to the gas chambers immediately. I saw another SS solider grab the baby by the legs. The crying had bothered him. He smashed the baby's head against the iron side of a truck until it was silent.'[18]

The incident was repeated at Groening's trial ten years later, a trial in which he admitted moral responsibility. The court found him guilty of being an accessory to mass murder, and sentenced him to four years in prison. In *Ashes to Ashes* Pinter's Rebecca channels the horrors of recent history and draws together the impulses to animate memory seen across the playwright's work to offer a picture of witnessing that captures the horrific ironies of Groening's trial.

In 2015, as I write, Guillermo Reyes Rammsy, a former soldier in the Chilean army, has been arrested after confessing to a series of political murders in the aftermath of the 1973 coup. The element in the case that perhaps strikes the strongest resonance with Pinter's work is the fact that his confession to participation in the killing of eighteen prisoners came when he called a radio show, *Chacotero sentimental*, or 'Loving Betrayal', to talk about past failed love affairs. The past, and the separation of personal and private in it, blurred into an extraordinary perpetrator's confession in a 30-minute discussion during which the graphic description of crimes mingled with a self-defence of Rammsy's actions as a conscript – a defence repeatedly challenged by the programme's host. The confession, an apparent overwhelming of sustained indifference by memory, led to his arrest for two of the murders, and the investigation of his involvement in the others.[19]

Dusty's *Party Time* question, 'what's happened to Jimmy?', continued to ring around the salons, newspaper offices, legal chambers, and television studios in which the tug of war over the General was played out in the period after his arrest. Yet the politics of the situation made clear that the tangled threads of history left Britain in an awkward position in relation to the former dictator. Was it the case that, as Thatcher argued, Pinochet's acceptance of democracy and his standing aside on losing a vote on the country's future represented the culmination of a mature and reasoned programme to secure the nation's economic stability and democratic future after the dreadful turmoil of the Allende era and the repression that followed? Was Pinochet, Chile's Thatcher, allowing for the necessary violence that the comparatively backward position of 1970s Chile necessitated? Did Pinochet's assistance not save many British lives?

In 1974, a British stockbroker with dual Chilean national-
ity, William Beausire, was arrested by police at an airport in
Argentina. Transferred to Chile, he was taken to the head-
quarters of the DINA, the secret police. His sister and his
mother were also there, under interrogation. Beausire was
then transported to the DINA's secret detention centre, the
Villa Grimaldi, a nineteenth-century mansion in the suburbs
of Santiago. There he was tortured with electric shocks, was
hung in the air, and had sticks forced into his rectum. After
this he was moved to another interrogation centre, and in July
DINA agents were observed taking him away. He was never
seen again.

In the words of the English lawyer, Geoffrey Bindman,
who mounted a civil case on behalf of Beausire's family in
the 1990s, Beausire was a fairly conservative businessman, and
was generally in favour of the regime.[20] It appears that his
sister, an opponent, was living with the deposed President
Allende's nephew and that Beausire was picked up for interrogation in order to discover the whereabouts of the nephew.
Beausire's case involved collusion between Argentinian and
Chilean juntas to disappear a man whose relationship to any
political cause was as tentative as being a relative of a dissenter.
'Where's William?' was a question being asked of Chile, and of
Pinochet, as he stood in the doorway of his Wentworth mansion. Other British victims of Pinochet's regime, including
the doctor Sheila Cassidy, whose detention without trial and
torture in the Villa Grimaldi during the Chilean coup had
long been a *cause célèbre* of human rights activists, might have
stood in for the Spanish victims whose fate was the subject
of Garzon's indictment, although it was a civil case that was
being brought by Beausire's solicitor's family. The tendrils of
the ruthless suppression of dissent stretched through the years

and across borders into the grounds of Pinochet's temporary home, and for a time the rule of international law seemed about to do that 'recognition' thing that Pinter described. The legal fate of Pinochet hung in the balance for over a year until finally the Home Secretary, Jack Straw, dismissed a decision by the Law Lords requiring his extradition on the grounds of the dictator's declining health. The General left Britain for home on a Chilean air force jet from a Lincolnshire airfield in March 2000. Yet his triumphant return to his supporters was not an end to the legal process. The see-sawing proceedings continued, finally resulting in Pinochet's house arrest on a series of charges in his 90th year. He died in 2006, the shadows of prosecution still hanging over him, the most recent indictment being complicity in the death of two of Allende's bodyguards in the days immediately after the coup. As the International Criminal Tribunal for the Former Yugoslavia and other tribunals have shown, international justice in cases of administrative torture and massacre may be said to move at a glacial pace, but there is something of the magnitude and weight of the glacier that renders it a powerful focus of attention.

In subsequent years the force of international law has been felt in a range of private settings: Charles Taylor's compound in Liberia, Slobodan Milošević's home in Belgrade, Radovan Karadžić's flat in Belgrade where he lived as an holistic healer, the small village house in which Ratko Mladić hid when his network of support had begun to crumble. In none of these cases is the scale of power an assurance of security from such jeopardy. The clubs, the buildings, the networks of shared interest, the languages and concerns of the assembled do not allow for those accused of wild abuses of power to remain secluded, and the language of the elite is no protection from the intrusions of a harsh and uncomfortable reality. Justice may not be faced, may be problematized, may be struck down, but impunity in such international cases no longer ensures that the remote hand of oppression remains as free from the consequences of its action as it had appeared to be, in Chile, in 1973.

In 2005 Harold Pinter gave a speech of acceptance on receiving the Nobel Prize for literature. In it he declared:

> In 1958 I wrote the following:
>> 'There are no hard distinctions between what is real and what is unreal, nor between what is true and what is false. A thing is not necessarily either true or false; it can be both true and false.'
>
>> I believe that these assertions still make sense and do still apply to the exploration of reality through art. So as a writer I stand by them but as a citizen I cannot. As a citizen I must ask: What is true? What is false?[21]

Perhaps this statement indicates a differentiation for Pinter between the responsibilities of the writer and those of the citizen that answers back to the questions raised by Prentice and Milne. The writer's commitment is to a dramatic image, the citizen's to a political engagement, and the final form and shape that each role takes are decided by context and circumstance – and perhaps by the desire to make a dramatic intervention. In the same speech Pinter went on to attack American foreign policy in relation to a number of historic circumstances up to the invasion of Iraq in 2004, and he suggested that President Bush and Prime Minister Blair should both be indicted by the UN court in order to stand trial for their actions in fomenting conflict. One might well feel that the situation is more complex than that. But I'd defend the right of Pinter to say it, to make the moral case clear and hang the consequences, to not just shut up and enjoy the hospitality.

In his speech Pinter also quoted at length from the Nobel Prize-winning Chilean poet Pablo Neruda's 'I'm Explaining a Few Things', a commentary on the Spanish Civil War. In November 2015 the Chilean government announced that Neruda's body was to be exhumed in order to establish whether he had, as suspected, died at the hands of Pinochet's secret police in the immediate aftermath of the 1973 coup.[22] At the time, Neruda, a supporter of Allende's government, was declared to have died in hospital from cancer. His sudden hospitalisation and death had long been viewed as suspicious, and now circumstances indicate that this was indeed a work of political disappearance, a dissenting voice silenced in order for the powerful to remain undisturbed. That after such a passage of time the case remains open is testimony to the power of writing, poetic and dramatic, to keep principled positions visible, speaking back to the abuse of power.

Unlike the case of Neruda's fate, the civil prosecution against Pinochet for involvement in the torture and disappearance of William Beausire was never resolved. After the General's death, Beausire's sister Diana, herself a victim of torture at the Villa Grimaldi, continued to try to establish what happened to him.[23] The question about the whereabouts of a brother asked by her dramatic avatar, Dusty, throughout *Party Time* remains the kind of question that troubles power and asserts the principles of the persistent pursuit of justice for victims. *Party Time*'s triumphant, squabbling, haunted, evasive figures are a study in the absurdist impossibility of silencing dissent, and the play is a compelling dramatic assertion of its power.

Notes

1   That the cruiser was 'sailing away' is the subject of a dispute. A British intelligence report subsequently released suggested that it had been ordered to move to a rendezvous elsewhere in the total exclusion zone.

2   The makers of the BBC Television motoring show *Top Gear* were accused of inflaming Argentinian public opinion leading to an international incident by driving a car with the number plate H982FKL – supposed reference to the conflict – during a shoot in the country. The situation became dangerous for presenters and crew as they attempted to leave the country, their vehicles being pelted with rocks before they crossed the border into Chile. A. Williams, 'Controversial *Top Gear* Number Plate WASN'T a Reference to Falklands War, Rules BBC Trust as It Rejects Complaints over Argentina "Prank"', *Mail Online*, 28 May 2016, www.dailymail.co.uk/news/article-3100892/Controversial-Gear-number-plate-WASN-T-reference-Falklands-War-rules-BBC-Trust-rejects-complaints-Argentina-prank.html (accessed 26 November 2015).

3   J. Baker, 'Grandson Lost in Dirty War is Found', *The Times*, 9 November 2015, p. 41. The article deals with the story of 'Martin', the grandson of Delia Giovanola. He was born in a secret detention centre in 1976 to Jorge Oscar Ogando and Stella Maris Montesano. Martin's parents have never been found and are believed to have been murdered in detention. In 2011, his sister, Virginia, who had been rescued by neighbours on the night of her parents' arrest, committed suicide after many unsuccessful years searching for her brother.

4   As I write, the UK parliament has voted to support airstrikes against the forces of the self-declared Islamic State of Syria and the Levant (ISIL), with the Shadow Foreign Minister of the opposition Labour Party, Hilary Benn, supporting the government motion for intervention in a fiery speech that characterises ISIL, accurately, as fascist.

5   B. Willis, ed., *Six Masters of the Spanish Sonnet* (Carbondale, IL: Southern Illinois University Press, 1993), p. 191, quoting Jorge Luis Borges, *Time*, 14 February 1983.

6   A senior investigating magistrate in the Spanish Supreme Court, Garzon was later convicted of illegally obtaining evidence through wiretapping and suspended from legal duties for eleven years. He currently works as the head of WikiLeaks founder Julian Assange's legal team.

7   M. Thatcher, 'Pinochet was this Country's Staunch, True Friend', speech to the Conservative Party Conference Fringe, *Guardian*, 6 October 1999, www.theguardian.com/world/1999/oct/06/pinochet.chile (accessed 9 November 2015).

8   T. Gibb, 'Lamont Gets Pinochet Medal', *Guardian*, 5 October 2000, www.theguardian.com/world/2000/dec/05/pinochet.chile (accessed 17 May 2016).

9   H. Pinter, *Independent*, 10 December 1998, www.independent.co.uk/news/the-pinochet-decision-that-he-will-be-made-to-face-his-past-is-uplifting-1190353.html (accessed 9 November 2015).

10 A. Fraser, *Must You Go? My Life with Harold Pinter* (London: Weidenfeld and Nicolson, 2010), p. 208.

11 Beckett, *Pinochet in Piccadilly* (London: Faber, 2002), p. 232.

12 P. O'Brien and J. Roddick, *Chile: The Pinochet Decade* (London: Latin American Bureau, 1983) offered a critical account of this economic experiment in its immediate aftermath.

13 J. Walsh, 'That Nice Mr Pinter', *Independent*, 8 February 1999, www.independent.co.uk/arts-entertainment/that-nice-mr-pinter-1069451.html (accessed 9 November 2015).

14 M. Billington, *The Life and Work of Harold Pinter* (London: Faber, 1996), p. 334.

15 P. Prentice, *The Pinter Ethic: The Erotic Aesthetic*, 2nd edn (London: Routledge, 2002), p. cxi.

16 D. Milne, 'Pinter's Sexual Politics' in P. Raby, *The Cambridge Companion to Harold Pinter* (Cambridge: Cambridge University Press, 2012), pp. 233–48 (p. 239).

17 H. Pinter, *Ashes to Ashes* (1996), in *Plays 4*, pp. 389–483 (p. 419).

18 M. Geyer, trans. C. Sultan, 'An SS Officer Remembers: The Bookkeeper from Auschwitz', *Der Spiegel*, 9 July 2005, www.spiegel.de/international/spiegel/an-ss-officer-remembers-the-bookkeeper-from-auschwitz-a-355188.html (accessed 13 March 2015).

19 J. Franklin, 'Former Chilean Soldier Charged with Murder after Stunning Radio Confession', *Guardian*, 11 December 2015, www.theguardian.com/world/2015/dec/11/former-chilean-soldier-charged-murder-radio-confession (accessed 14 December 2015).

20 'Briton William Beausire "Returns" to Haunt Pinochet', *BBC News*, 26 October 1998, http://news.bbc.co.uk/1/hi/special_report/1998/10/98/the_pinochet_file/201678.stm (accessed 9 November 2015).

21 H. Pinter, 'Art, Truth and Politics' (2005), www.nobelprize.org/nobel_prizes/literature/laureates/2005/pinter-lecture-e.html (accessed 9 November 2015).

22 'Chile Admits Pablo Neruda Might Have Been Murdered by Pinochet Regime', *Guardian*, 6 November 2015, www.theguardian.com/books/2015/nov/06/chile-admits-pablo-neruda-might-have-been-murdered-by-pinochet-regime (accessed 9 November 2015).

23 N. Belton, *The Good Listener. Helen Bamber: A Life against Cruelty*, 2nd edn (London: Faber, 2012). The chapter 'Poor Ghost', pp. 229-66, is a disturbing narrative of Beausire's imprisonment and final days, compiled from accounts of those who came across him in captivity.

Index

References to endnotes consist of the page number followed by the letter 'n' followed by the number of the note.

20 June writers' group 20, 35, 43

abstracted realism 51
Allende, Salvador 7, 9, 13, 57, 58, 59, 61
Almeida theatre, Islington, London 4
Amnesty International 9
Arden, John 52
Argentina: 1976–78 events and Pinter's *One for the Road* 10–14; Falklands War (1982) 43–5, 57; Mothers of the Plaza de Mayo 44, 47; and William Beausire case 58
'Arthur Miller's Socks' (essay, Harold Pinter) 2
Ashcroft, Peggy 7
Ashes to Ashes (Harold Pinter) 20, 54–6
Auerbach, Frank 28

Bacon, Francis 28
BBC Television: 1980 production of *The Caretaker* 14–15; Pinter and Lamont on Pinochet's arrest on *Newsnight* 50; *The Young Ones* (sitcom) 44
Beausire, Diana 61
Beausire, William 58–9, 61
Beckett, Andy 9, 13–14
Belarus Free Theatre, Minsk 22
Benn, Hilary 62n4
Berlin Wall, fall of 3, 35
Betrayal (Harold Pinter) 5, 7
Billington, Michael 7, 52, 53
Bindman, Geoffrey 58
The Birthday Party (Harold Pinter) 5, 6, 14, 30
Blair, Tony 47, 60
Bond, Edward 52
Borges, Jorge Luis 45

Brown, Craig 20–1
Browning, Robert, *A Toccata of Galuppi's* 15
Buñuel, Luis 52
Bush, George W. 60

The Caretaker (Harold Pinter) 5, 26; 1980 BBC TV production 14–15
Cassidy, Sheila 58
Ceaușescu, Nikolai 3–4
Chiasson, Basil 41n3
'Chicago Boys' 50
Chile: 1973 coup 7–9, 13–14; Chilean government and Pinochet's arrest in UK 47; and Falklands War (1982) 45; Guillermo Reyes Rammsy case 57; Pablo Neruda case 61; William Beausire case 58–9, 61
China, human rights and trade deals 2
clubs, literal and metaphorical 36–9
Conservative Party (UK): Thatcher administration 35, 44; Thatcher's Pinochet speech at 1999 conference 48
Costa-Gavras: *Missing* 7–8, 9; *Music Box* 8
Cranham, Kenneth 14

dissent: dissenting voices in *Party Time* 29, 32–4, 61; *see also* political engagement
drama, and power 2
Dylan, Bob 9

Eastern Europe, 1989 revolutions 3–4

Faber Collected Plays 4 volume (Harold Pinter) 20
Falklands War (1982) 43–5, 57
fascism 36, 44, 62n4
Fraser, Antonia 15

Gaieties Cricket Club 37
Galtieri, General Leopold 44–5
Garzon, Balthazar 47, 58
Germany: Berlin Wall, fall of 3, 35; Nuremburg trials 51; Oskar Groening trial 56; Pinter's Shakespeare prize speech (1970) 4–5
Geyer, Matthias 56
Good Friday Agreement (1998) 51
Gordon, Robert 19
Gray, Simon 15
Groening, Oskar 56

Havel, Václav 7
Hern, Nick 6
'hollowness' 38
The Homecoming (Harold Pinter) 5
Horman, Charles 8
Horman, Ed 7, 8
Horman, Joyce 7, 8
human rights: and Amnesty International 9; and Pinter's writing 4, 21; and trade deals

with China 2; Universal
Declaration of Human
Rights (United Nations) 49
Hussein, Saddam 17, 18–19

incident at dinner: American
Embassy in Turkey inci-
dent 1–2, 7; background
and main theme of Pinter's
Party Time 2–4; Chile and
1973 coup 7–9, 13–14;
Pinteresque style 5–6;
Pinter's *One for the Road*
and political events in
Argentina (1976-78) 10–14;
Pinter's political engagement 4–5, 6–7, 9; Pinter's
political engagement and
Mountain Language 14, 15–20;
Pinter's political engagement and post-*Mountain
Language* work 20–1; Pinter's
reputation and impact 20–
2; techniques of Pinter's
dramaturgy 14–15
The Independent: Pinter interview on Pinochet case and
international law 51; Pinter's
article on Pinochet's UK
arrest 49
International Criminal
Tribunal for the Former
Yugoslavia 51, 59
international law/justice 49,
51, 58–60
Iraq: Kurdish conflict 17, 18–
19; Pinter on Iraq war
(2004) 60–1

ISIL (Islamic State of Syria and
the Levant) 43, 62n4

Jara, Victor 9

Kane, Sarah 20
Karadžić, Radovan 59
Kurds: Kurdish conflicts 17–19;
Pinter's *Mountain Language*
and arrest of émigré Kurds in
London 21–2

Labour Party (UK), 'ethical'
foreign policy and Pinochet's
detention 47
Lamont, Norman 48–9, 50
language: and meaning 28, 37;
and national identity 18;
poetic estrangement of 30;
and power 3, 21, 22; *see also
Mountain Language* (Harold
Pinter)
Larkin, Philip 15
Lemmon, Jack 7
London, city of clubs 36–7
Lyric Studio, Hammersmith,
London 11

McGrath, John 52
Madison Square Garden Victor
Jara concert (1974) 9
Marylebone Cricket Club 37
memory: and *Ashes to Ashes* 54–
7; and *Party Time* 28, 32, 38
Mercer, David 7
Miller, Arthur 1–2; *The
Crucible* 2
Milne, Drew 19, 51, 53–4, 60

Milošević, Slobodan 59
Missing (Costa-Gavras) 7–8, 9
Mitchell, Warren 14
Mladić, Ratko 59
Mothers of the Plaza de
    Mayo 44, 47
Mountain Language (Harold
    Pinter) 4, 14, 15–20,
    21–2, 40

National Student Drama
    Festival (UK, 1962), Pinter's
    speech 6
Neruda, Pablo 61
Newsnight (BBC Television),
    Pinter and Lamont on
    Pinochet's arrest 50
The New World Order (Harold
    Pinter) 20, 40
Nobel Prize for litera-
    ture (2005) 21; Pinter's
    speech 60–1
No Man's Land (Harold Pinter)
    5, 7, 26, 43
nostalgia, and power games
    31–2, 35
Nuremburg trials 51

Old Times (Harold Pinter)
    5, 7, 43
One for the Road (Harold
    Pinter) 4, 6–7, 11–13, 17,
    18, 22, 40
overstatement, tone of 29–30

Party Time (Harold Pinter):
    1991 premiere (Almeida
    theatre, London) 4; 'All you
have to do is shut up and
    enjoy the hospitality' 1, 28;
    background and main
    theme 2–4; clubs, literal and
    metaphorical 36–9; compari-
    son with earlier plays 25–6;
    critique of right-wing power
    35–6, 52–3; dissenting voices
    29, 32–4, 61; 'hollowness' 38;
    memory 28, 32, 38; nostalgia
    and power games 31–2, 35;
    overstatement, tone of 29–30;
Pinteresque style 28;
powerful men vs subordinated
    women 26–8, 33–4, 52–3;
    satiric take on Thatcher
    administration 35; victims 40;
    'What's happened to
    Jimmy?' 3, 26, 31, 34,
    39–40, 57, 61; women and
    agency 53–4
PEN International 1, 7
Pinochet, Augusto 7, 8–9,
    13–14, 45–51, 57, 58–9, 61
Pinter, Harold: American
    Embassy in Turkey inci-
    dent 1–2, 7; 'clubbable' 37;
    Holland Park residence 43;
    on Iraq war (2004) 60–1;
    National Student Drama
    Festival speech (1962) 6;
    Nobel Prize for literature 21;
    Nobel Prize for literature
    acceptance speech 60–1;
    and PEN International 1, 7;
    on Pinochet case and
    international law 49, 51, 59;
    political engagement

4–5, 6–7, 9, 14, 15–21;
reputation and impact 20–2;
Shakespeare prize speech
(West Germany, 1970) 4–5;
'The weasel under the
cocktail cabinet' quote 5, 6;
'What I write has no obliga-
tion to anything other than
itself' quote 6; on writer's
vs citizen's responsibilities
60; see also Pinteresque style;
Pinter's works
Pinteresque style 5–6, 28;
techniques of Pinter's
dramaturgy 14–15
Pinter's works: 'Arthur Miller's
Socks' (essay) 2; Ashes to Ashes
20, 54–6; Betrayal 5, 7; The
Birthday Party 5, 6, 14, 30;
The Caretaker 5, 14–15, 26;
Faber Collected Plays 4 volume 20; The Homecoming 5;
Mountain Language 4, 14,
15–20, 21–2, 40; The New
World Order 20, 40; No Man's
Land 5, 7, 26, 43; Old Times
5, 7, 43; One for the Road 4,
6–7, 11–13, 17, 18, 22, 40;
The Room 5; 'Writing for the
Theatre' (Collected Plays) 6;
see also Party Time (Harold
Pinter)
political engagement 4–5, 6–7,
9, 14, 15–21; see also dissent
power: and drama 2; and
language 3, 21, 22; and
nostalgia 31–2, 35; right-
wing power, critique of 35–6,

52–3; see also dissent; political
engagement
Prentice, Penelope 53, 60
Pryce, Jonathan 14

Rammsy, Guillermo Reyes 57
rape, as weapon of terror 52–3
The Room (Harold Pinter) 5
Roumania, 1989
revolution 3–4
Rueda, Sergio 13–14

Scherban, Vladimir 22
Shakespeare, William,
King Lear 2
Shakespeare prize (West
Germany), Pinter's 1970
speech 4–5
Sophocles, Antigone 2
South Africa: end of
Apartheid 35; Truth
and Reconciliation
Commission 51
Spacek, Sissy 7, 8
Der Spiegel, Matthias Geyer's
interview of Oskar
Groening 56
Straw, Jack 47, 59
Syria, and ISIL (Islamic State
of Syria and the Levant)
43, 62n4

Taylor, Charles 59
Thatcher, Margaret 35, 42–3,
44, 45–6, 47–8, 50, 57
The Times, on 118th child
kidnapped by Argentinian
junta 44

Turkey: American Embassy incident 1–2, 7; Kurdish insurgency 17–19

Universal Declaration of Human Rights (United Nations) 49

victims: of oppressive regimes and international law 58–60; in Pinter's plays 40

Wardle, Irving 4, 28
'The weasel under the cocktail cabinet' (Pinter's quote) 5, 6
Wentworth days: description of Wentworth Estate 42–3; Falklands War (1982) 43–5, 57; Pinochet and Thatcher meeting at Wentworth 45–6, 47–8; Pinochet case 46–9, 57, 58–9; Pinter on Pinochet's arrest and international law 49–50, 51, 59; Pinter's critique of right-wing power in *Party Time* 52–3; Pinter's female characters 53–4; Pinter's final play *Ashes to Ashes* and memory 54–7; Pinter's Nobel Prize acceptance speech 60–1; victims of oppressive regimes and international law 58–60
women: powerful men vs subordinated women 26–8, 33–4, 52–3; women's oppression and agency 53–4
World Cup (1978) 10, 11
'Writing for the Theatre' (*Collected Plays*, Harold Pinter) 6

Xi, Jinping 2

The Young Ones (BBC television) 44
Yugoslavia: International Criminal Tribunal for the Former Yugoslavia 51, 59; Yugoslav Civil War (1990s) 19–20